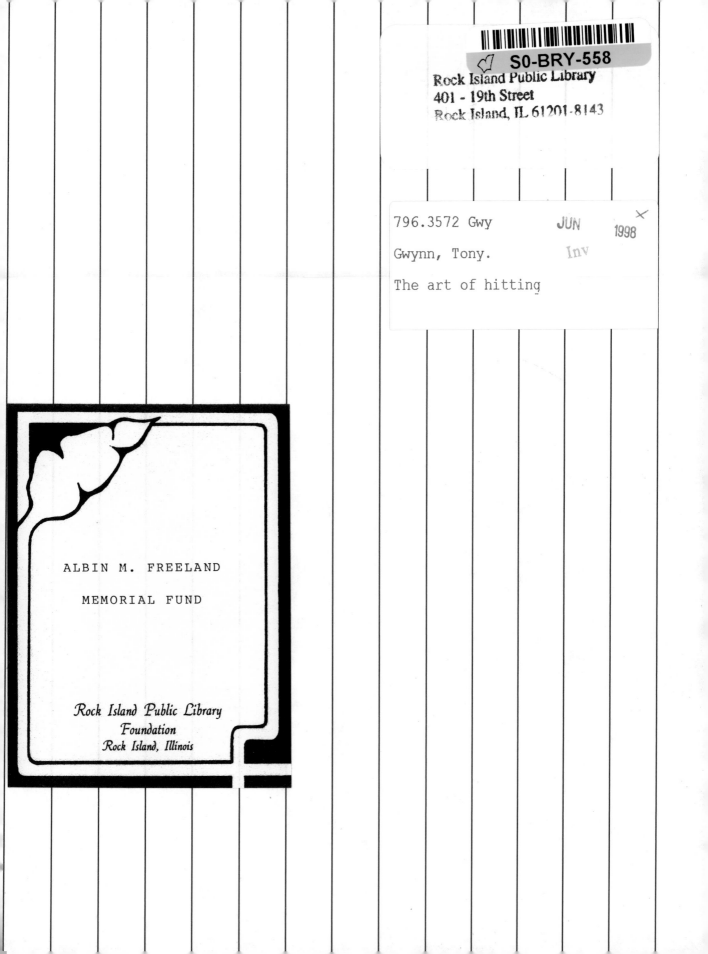

ALBIN M. FREELAND

MEMORIAL FUND

Rock Island Public Library
Foundation
Rock Island, Illinois

TONY GWYNN

The Art of Hitting

TONY GWYNN

The Art of Hitting

WITH ROGER VAUGHAN

FOREWORD BY TED WILLIAMS

GT
PUBLISHING
NEW YORK

ACKNOWLEDGMENTS

Thanks to Leslie Stoker, for putting it all together; to Howard Klein, for the look; to Kippy Requardt, for improving my game; to Alexandra Truitt and Jerry Marshall, for ace picture research; to Stuart Hothem, the answer man; and to Tony and Alicia, for the ride. RV

Text copyright © 1998 Tony Gwynn

All rights reserved. Reproduction in whole or in part without express written permission of the publisher is prohibited.

Picture credits are on page 144.

Published in 1998 by GT Publishing Corporation
16 East 40th Street
New York, NY 10016

DESIGN BY HOWARD KLEIN

Photo Editor: Alexandra Truitt ◆ Photo Researcher: Jerry Marshall

Library of Congress Cataloging-in-Publication Data

Gwynn, Tony.
The art of hitting / Tony Gwynn with Roger Vaughan ; foreword by Ted Williams.
p.   cm.
ISBN 1-57719-347-4
1. Batting (Baseball)   I. Vaughan, Roger.   II. Title.
GV869.G99   1998
796.357'27—dc21   98-12165
CIP

Printed in the United States of America

2 4 6 8 10 9 7 5 3 1

First printing

I don't like to compare myself to hitters of the past because people always start talking about eras—"Gwynn's got to face four different pitchers in a game"—all that stuff. Forget all that. It's still the game of baseball. When I'm dead and gone, all that will be left is the numbers. They won't remember how much heart a person had, or how consistent he was, they'll just look at the numbers. And the numbers will tell them that I won eight batting titles; that I tied Honus Wagner for winning the most. The numbers will tell them that Wagner was a .345 lifetime hitter, and that I am a .340 lifetime hitter. So who was better? Honus Wagner. That's how it will be judged.

TONY GWYNN

CONTENTS

I AM A GREAT ADMIRER of Tony Gwynn, as a hitter and as a person. I've said for a long time that if any current major league player is going to hit .400, Tony is the most likely. He made a pretty good run at it in 1994, hitting .394. I still think that of all the hitters I've watched, he has the best chance.

Tony's style of hitting is quite different from mine, but we have a good deal in common, too. We both grew up in Southern California—he's from Long Beach, I'm from San Diego—and don't underestimate the importance of that. I've always said that a young ballplayer can have no greater luck than to grow up in a place where you can practice and play every day, year-round. For a young hitter, there's no substitute for practicing until you have calluses on your hands.

That's another similarity between Tony and me. We both love to hit. We love everything about it. Hitting is not only our profession, it's our passion. We like to talk about it, read about it, study it, analyze it, break it down to it's component parts and then put it back together in the batting cage and at the plate. There's nothing like testing your theories with a million swings. No young hitter of my era practiced more than I did, and I'm pretty sure that no hitter today works at his craft harder than Tony Gwynn.

It helps to be smart, and Tony is. He understands his swing and the mental chess game between the pitcher and the hitter. Every bit of knowledge you have can be an advantage. You need to watch batting practice. You need to study pitchers. You need to know patterns and percentages. I used to talk to good hitters all the time, picking their brains, starting when I first broke in with the Pacific Coast League San Diego Padres in 1936–37.

Tony is that way, too. He's always asking questions, studying videotapes, trying to improve. I'm flattered that he read my book, *The Science of Hitting*, and said it helped him, just as I know his book is going to help a lot of young hitters. I'm delighted to say that Tony Gwynn is as great a guy as he is a hitter. I'm proud that he has played his whole career in my hometown, San Diego, and the people there just love him.

Tony and I have had a couple long talks about hitting, and I've enjoyed them immensely. We're different, though. His favorite pitch to hit is from the middle of the plate out, and he likes to go to left field with it. I was a dead pull hitter most of my career, which is why Lou Boudreau devised "the Williams Shift" and put three infielders on the right side of the diamond against me. It was only late in my career that I started to hit more to left field.

But when we talked, I told Tony that major league history is made on the inside part of the plate, and I know he took that to heart. He told me the next time I saw him that he hit his first career grand slam in Philadelphia, putting that nice, easy swing of his on an inside pitch and pulling it out of the park. In 1997, he not only won his eighth batting title but also set career highs for home runs and runs batted in. Tony is the consummate con-

tact hitter, but he's not a "singles hitter." He can drive the ball. And even though he is hitting with more power now, he is still the toughest guy in the major leagues to strike out, and he's a terrific two-strike hitter.

We talked a lot about the subtleties and nuances of hitting, but one thing I said to Tony was: Don't change your swing. That was the best advice I ever got. The first time I met Lefty O'Doul, who was a great major league player and a legend in the Pacific Coast League when I broke in, I asked him for some advice. He said, "Kid, don't let anybody change your swing." In retrospect, that was maybe the biggest compliment I ever got.

Tony has a great swing. He knows it. He's analyzed what works for him. He has also made himself a better hitter by understanding the mechanics and the thought processes that go into it. I still believe that hitting is a science, and the more we understand about it and practice what we learn, the better we get. Tony Gwynn does that, which is why I still think he might hit .400 one of these years.

TED WILLIAMS, 1998

INTRODUCTION

HE PLAN WAS *to drive across the country to San Diego.*

Alicia Gwynn and her husband, Tony Gwynn, who hits baseballs at a .340 (lifetime) clip

for a living, had been relaxing in Indianapolis at their vacation home since the San

Diego Padres' lackluster 1997 season had ended in October. The only thing remarkable

about the Padres' season was Tony Gwynn's performance. The 37-year-old Gwynn had 220 hits, 119 RBIs, and a .372 average that brought him his eighth National League Batting Championship (a record he now shares with Honus Wagner); his preposterously small number of strikeouts totaled just 28 in nearly 600 at-bats. He was a little miffed about the strikeouts. In 1996, while batting .353, he struck out only 17 times.

Gwynn is one of the greatest pure hitters in the history of baseball. He has hit over .350 in six seasons, and logged over 200 hits a season five times. In a time when professional sports seems to have eschewed the category, Gwynn is also a

gentleman of the game of baseball.

Tony told me over the phone that he and Alicia would first drive to Nashville to see his grandmother, then head west, stopping at Kansas City to give a hitting clinic. Kansas City was on the way, more or less, he said, and they had a lot of stuff to take home. Plus, well—frankly—they both hated to fly. He had to fly during the season, of course, but he had the whole team to buoy him up, get him through the ordeal. But never would he fly for pleasure.

We met at the airport in Nashville at 3 P.M. on a Saturday afternoon in October, and started driving to Kansas City, 600 miles away. Gwynn's appearance at the hitting clinic was in support of friend and

ALICIA DRIVES, TONY TALKS.

Padres teammate Terry Shumpert, who was using the occasion to introduce his baseball camp. The clinic was scheduled for Sunday afternoon. Facing a 600-mile drive beginning mid-afternoon didn't seem to faze the Gwynns in the least. Alicia was asleep in the back after ten miles. Tony surfed the AM dial until he found

ESPN radio, then sat back and gave the big black Ford Expedition its head.

We arrived in Kansas City at 2:30 A.M. and checked into a hotel, slept late. Shumpert showed up around 1:00 P.M., and we followed his van for an hour, driving beyond the suburbs to the compact, treeless campus of Longview Community

College where the clinic was being held. There were about 100 people—young boys, fathers, mothers, a few young girls —all seated in bleachers adjoining a basketball court. After a short introduction by Shumpert, Tony Gwynn stepped up with a Gwynn-model Louisville Slugger bat in hand. It bore the "Gwynn finish": barrel painted black with an unpainted, sanded handle. He had on his traveling clothes: black and white cross-trainers; black sweat pants; black T-shirt; black cap ("No Fear" embroidered in black), with sunglasses propped above the bill. He handed the bat to a boy at one end of the bleachers and told him to have a look and pass it around. Then he addressed the gathering in a sharp, clear voice that was a combination of rapper, military instructor, and stand-up comedian.

"Hitting, what I do, is really pretty simple. You see the ball, then you hit the ball. You get up to the plate, the pitcher gets ready, you land soft on the front foot, get your hands to the hitting position, bring the knob of the bat to the ball, and follow through. That's it. Any questions?"

The response, a mixture of laughter and applause, was spontaneous, heartfelt, and charged with anticipation. Tony Gwynn isn't only the best hitter in baseball since Ted Williams, he's accessible, funny, easy going, and a good guy. It took less than a minute for the audience to figure that out. And here he was at Longview Community College, somewhere in the middle of Kansas, giving it the full Broadway treatment, ready to share his hitting techniques with anyone who wanted to pay attention. It was a lucky day at Longview.

ROGER VAUGHAN, 1998

Contact!

T HE 1997 SEASON *was important for Tony Gwynn. He had had Achilles tendon surgery after the 1996 season, and the talk started about how age combined with injuries could result in lowered performance. Most disturbing of all, Gwynn could hear it coming from his own front office.*

I learned a lot the winter of 1996 because I had to change the way I do things. Rehabilitation for Achilles surgery involves running. Whereas in years past, because of knee surgeries I'd ride the bike or get on a treadmill or StairMaster, this past winter I had to run.

The situation made me remember something Padres infielder Fred Lynn had told me a few years back. He was in his mid-thirties at the time. I asked him one day how he kept up. He said he had to work harder at it, and that was about it. I knew

TONY GWYNN READY TO HIT: WEIGHT BALANCED, FRONT FOOT DOWN SOFTLY, HANDS IN THE COCKED POSITION.

even then I had to work harder because I'm not built like your typical athlete.

I had to wait until the middle of January for the Achilles to heal enough to run on. Then For a good solid month I was running every day, and it really made a difference in the way I went about my business. I could feel I had snap in my bat that I hadn't had the year before.

The first time the issue of hitting .400 came up was during spring training. I was talking to our minor leaguers, and somebody asked me what kind of things I expected to do this year. I said, "Well, I'm in the best shape of my life, I've worked really hard, and if I stay healthy, I might make a run at it." And I didn't say it

TOP: GOING TO WORK AT SPRING TRAINING, PEORIA, ARIZONA. THE LOCKER ROOM IS A LONG WALK, SO GWYNN CARRIES EXTRA BATS, GLOVES, SHOES, IN A SHOULDER BAG. ABOVE: AS HE GETS OLDER, GWYNN WORKS HARDER TO STAY IN SHAPE. LEFT: MAKING CONTACT. FOLLOWING PAGES: GWYNN COMING OUT OF THE BOX AFTER LINING A DOUBLE AT DODGER STADIUM. CATCHER MIKE PIAZZA WATCHES IT GO.

straight out, but I meant I might make a run at doing something that hadn't been done in a long time. I was talking about hitting .400.

I didn't come into the 1997 season thinking I could hit .400, but I did think I was going to have one of my best years because of how hard I had worked. Then three weeks into the season, there I was at .400. I wondered if it was possible.

I had a conversation with Ted Williams two years ago and we talked about hitting .400. He was trying to convince me that if anybody in today's game would do it, it would be me. I said, "You know Mr. Williams, I appreciate that but I know how difficult hitting .400 is. I had a little taste of it in 1994, and I know." And he said, "Tony, let me tell you something, if I knew people were going to be making such a big deal out of hitting .400 today, I'd have done it more often." I laughed, but then when I thought about it, in his era he hit .406 and other players had done it pretty recently before him.

"WE ALL PRACTICE SPRINTING OUT OF THE BATTER'S BOX AFTER MAKING CONTACT. THAT'S HOW OUTS BECOME HITS, AND SINGLES BECOME DOUBLES."

From Ted's way of thinking, he probably could have done it a few more times. It wasn't that big a deal to him. Because that .406 of his has stood the test of time, now it's amazing. It's a huge deal any time somebody makes a run at it.

Nothing excites the world of baseball more than the possibility of someone hitting .400. It's been so long since anyone has done it that the achievement has attained heroic status. After the four-minute mile fell, it kept on falling. And no-hitters occur regularly, at the rate of one or two per season. But hitting .400 has remained unattainable for all but a chosen few.

Ted Williams crossed the .400 barrier in 1941. The closest any player has come since then was .394, registered by Tony Gwynn in 1994.

Gwynn suggests that Williams was casual about his accomplishment because others had attained the magic number relatively close to his time. But the second-to-last player to hit .400 was Clark Terry, in 1930 (.401), when Ted Williams was 12 years old. One has to reach back to the 1920s before the .400 ranks get "crowded." Rogers Hornsby hit .403 in 1925, a veritable slump from his

ABOVE: TED WILLIAMS, THE LAST .400 HITTER, SHOWING HIS CLASSIC FOLLOW-THROUGH, WITH THE UPPER HAND STILL FIRMLY GRIPPING THE BAT. OPPOSITE: GWYNN CAME CLOSE IN 1994 WITH .394. FOLLOWING PAGES: GWYNN IS ONE OF THE FEW PLAYERS WHO ANSWERS FAN MAIL. "THE FANS HAVE BEEN GOOD TO ME. I THINK THEY RESPECT WHAT I DO."

1924 season in which he hit a whopping .424. In 1922, the incredible trio of Hornsby (.403), Ty Cobb (.401), and George Sisler (.420) joined the exclusive club, although Sisler had already become a member in 1920 (.407), and Cobb in 1911 (.420) and 1912 (.409).

What was it about the early 1920s that could produce six averages of .400-plus in half a decade; three men who would (among them) hit .400 or better six times in the course of five seasons?

Baseball historian and statistician, Craig Wright, says there are several reasons. First, a whiter ball. After Ray Chapman was killed by a pitch in 1920, umpires were told to change balls more

OPPOSITE: **The National League's 1997 MVP, Larry Walker of Colorado, displays the power that racked up 49 home runs.**
ABOVE: **Gwynn finesses a ball out front, pulling it to right. Both men hit off a stiff front leg, a sign of good balance.**

often. *Starting in 1918, balls were wrapped with Australian yarn that could be more heavily tensioned. So the ball became livelier. And in 1920, it became illegal for pitchers to apply any foreign*

substance to the ball. All these changes favored the hitter.

But the key reason averages soared in the 1920s, according to Wright, was that dead-ball-era hitting habits carried over. During dead-ball days, power wasn't a part of the hitter's game. Players put all their ability into hitting for average. In today's game, with the emphasis on the home run, hitters have to decide how much average they will sacrifice for power, and vice versa.

In any case, since 1941, only Gwynn

has come close. Wright says he did a "statistical chance" study some years ago that indicated Tony Gwynn had a 50-50 chance of hitting .400. "I didn't think it was possible in the modern game," Wright says, "but Tony Gwynn convinced me otherwise."

I guess many people thought if anybody was going to do it, it was going to be me. But even when I was hitting .400 in June, I knew how tough it was going to be to hit .400 in the long haul, and I really didn't think that I could do it. I didn't have that intangible thing going for me.

In order to hit .400 you have to walk a lot, or get hit by the pitcher a lot, or hit a ton of sacrifice volume. You've got to nullify some of your at-bats in order to make a really good run at it. And there was nothing in my game that was going to allow me to nullify the at-bats. Whereas Larry Walker, for example, might have a better shot at it because he walks a lot. People pitch around him because he can hit the ball out of the ballpark.

GWYNN FOLLOWS THROUGH AFTER BANGING ONE INTO HIS FAVORITE "5.5 HOLE" (BETWEEN SHORT STOP AND THIRD BASE) AGAINST HOUSTON.

Pitchers are going to take their chances with me because I don't hit a lot of home runs. I get my hits, but I was going to have to get 250 of them to make a real legitimate run at .400 because I didn't have those walks to count on. And 250 hits is a tall order.

Gwynn missed .400 by 28 points in 1997. It was the second-closest he's ever come to the magic number. He refers to the "taste of it" he had in 1994. That year, he only missed .400 by six points. It was the year of the baseball strike. He was hot when the strike was called, but he went out with everybody else. He felt he would have been over .400 by the end of September, but it wasn't to be. He stayed at .394, just six points away from certain immortality. It was more than good enough to win the batting championship—something of an anti-climax in a baseball year best forgotten.

In 1997, his .372 average brought Gwynn his eighth batting championship (better by six points than Colorado's Larry Walker). Tony's father and several other partisans said it should have been his ninth. In 1991, Gwynn nursed a sore knee most of the season. Shortly after he'd qualified for the batting title with

500 at-bats, the knee took a turn for the worse. He was batting .325 at the time. His father told him to quit for the season and have surgery, pointing out that the knee was worthless to him, and the Padres were out of the race anyway. Gwynn wouldn't do it. He felt he'd be accused of slipping in the back door if he won the title, taking the easy way out. He stayed in the lineup, finishing the season with a .317 average. Terry Pendleton won the title with an average of .319.

Jerry Coleman, the former Yankee infielder who broadcasts Padres games on the radio, is one of my greatest fans. Jerry agrees with my father that I should have won the batting title in 1991. He's one of those guys who tells me I could have played in any era—I could have played in his era, I could have played in Jackie Robinson's era. We'll never know. I just appreciate people saying kind things about me.

THE NATURAL

ANTHONY KEITH GWYNN *was born in Los Angeles on May 9, 1960, the middle brother of three. When he was ten, his parents moved the family to Long Beach. All three boys loved it there because they were sports crazy, and it was in Long Beach that they first started to play organized sports, including Little League.*

Both of Tony's parents worked, but arranged their schedules so one parent was always home. Tony's father managed a warehouse for the State of California during the day. His mother worked for the post office at night. Tony says they were strict by today's standards, "but you could throw in your two cents worth anytime."

Alicia, who grew up down the street from Tony, says her parents were much more strict. "My parents were elders of the church," she says, raising an eye-brow. "The only reason I got to date Tony is because my father knew the Gwynns. He told my mother they were good boys. If not for that I probably wouldn't have been able to date anybody until I was in college."

Alicia says she and Tony got to know each other because his team and her brother Eric's team were usually in the Little League championship game. St. Mark's Lions vs. the Long Beach Cubs. The rivalry was intense. "We had this little thing going on the sidelines," Alicia says, "yelling at each other. Eric was the catcher. Tony was an outfielder. When Tony got on base we'd be yelling, 'He's

TONY GWYNN IN 1987.

not gonna run on you.' I think Tony ran on Eric and he made it."

"He threw me out, Tony says. "That's why I never got to hear the end of it. I said he'd never throw me out. I'd see Alicia on the street coming home from school. She used to call me names, I'd call her names back. She'd taunt me, 'Yeah, he threw you out. Told you. Threw you out easy, too.'"

They began dating in high school. Up to then, the neighborhood sports rivalry between the two families was too intense for romance to bloom. With tongue only slightly in cheek, Alicia says Tony just kept coming at her. "I decided to give him a chance. I think we had a bet." Tony bet her that his own football team—the league champions—would lose their next game. Naturally, he lost the bet. The payoff was to take Alicia and her best friend to dinner.

Things worked out and progressed better than I had hoped. I knew all along that we were kind of compatible because

OPPOSITE: **GWYNN PLAYED POINT GUARD AT SAN DIEGO STATE, WHERE HE SET A RECORD FOR ASSISTS THAT STILL STANDS. ON THE BALL FIELD** (ABOVE), **HE HIT .423 AND .416 HIS JUNIOR AND SENIOR YEARS.**

she loved sports, too. When we were in high school they didn't have women's athletics like they do now, but she played flag football, volleyball, softball, and she ran track. She could fly.

One day after we'd started dating, we were out in front of her house and I told her I thought I could beat her. I knew she was fast, but I didn't know how fast. She dusted me off pretty quick. When Alicia does what she says she's gonna do, she just starts laughing. And she was laughing up a storm right there on the street.

Even though we were going out we were still very competitive.

At age 11, Tony Gwynn had a .500 average in Little League play. He recalls that sports came easy to him. Charles, his older brother, liked tennis and practiced a lot. When Charles couldn't find an opponent, he'd persuade Tony to play with him. Tony, who rarely picked up a racket, would always beat him, much to Charles's disgust.

One evening after a match, Charles was moping around the house, and my father took me aside. "You know what?" he told me, "You're just naturally athletic. Whatever it is you want to do, you can do it well." I didn't think much about it at the time, but as I got older I knew he was right.

One of my Little League coaches, Joe Parusho, was the first guy who ever broke down my swing and got me thinking about it. He had a scientific approach. At home, Charles and my dad got me into the mechanics of the swing. I read Ted Williams' *The Science of Hitting*, and we'd watch the Dodgers play on television— Ron Cey, Davey Lopes—and talk about the swing: hips, hands, get the front foot down, cock the hands, bat speed. I

thought about that stuff all the time, but I didn't begin working at baseball until the day I signed my major league contract. Charles was a power hitter; I was a contact hitter from the beginning.

In high school (Long Beach Poly) and college (San Diego State), I played basketball almost to the middle of baseball season, because the seasons overlap. I hit well in high school, and at San Diego State I hit .400 (.423 junior year; .416 as a senior). But I never worked at it because I wanted to take a crack at playing in the NBA. The truth was I was too short and too slow, despite having a record for assists at State that still stands. So I figured, hey, if I play baseball and I get my foot in the door, I might be able to play that game for a long time.

The month of June 1981, was a busy one for Tony Gwynn. He married Alicia on June 6, was drafted by the Padres on June 9, and signed his first major league contract on June 25. He says the day he signed his contract he decided he was going to start working at this sport that had come easy to him.

THE DODGERS' RON CEY, ONE OF GWYNN'S CHILDHOOD HEROES.

NEWLYWEDS TONY AND ALICIA GWYNN
ON JUNE 25,1981, THE DAY GWYNN
SIGNED WITH THE PADRES.

I decided I wasn't going to rely on natural ability like I always had. I was one of those guys who could do just enough to satisfy other people. Schoolwork, basketball, baseball, I always did just enough. But there's something about signing that contract—I suddenly realized that if this was my living, I needed to pay a lot more attention to it.

My mom and dad were workaholics, both of them. When I signed, all the things my parents told me about working hard came back to me. The day I signed I told Alicia that there were a lot of things I needed to learn. From that point on I dedicated myself to trying to be the best I could be.

The Padres organization sent me off to Walla Walla, Washington. I decided I was going to give myself three years to get to the big leagues, and if I couldn't get there in three years, then I was going to do something else.

In the Short-A League at Walla Walla, I hit like I had in college. There were more breaking balls and changeups, and I was frankly surprised I kept hitting at a good clip. In college, we used aluminum bats; in Walla Walla, I had to change to a wood bat. That was a big adjustment. If you get jammed [a strike on the extreme inside of the plate] using an aluminum bat, you can still hit a bullet off the handle. It's not the same with wood. My first batting practice, I connected with a ball inside on the handle and it really hurt.

When I arrived at Walla Walla the major leagues were on strike, so a lot of

THE DODGERS' DAVEY LOPES, ANOTHER
OF GWYNN'S CHILDHOOD HEROS.

the players went off on the circuit, visiting the farm teams. I got a chance to talk with guys like Bobby Tolan and Frank Howard and I learned a lot. I'd get to the park early every day and try to find somebody to throw me extra batting practice. It's hot on the field, and a lot of guys didn't want to go out early. But with the majors on strike there was always somebody around. I'd come into the clubhouse and guys like Terry Kennedy, Rick Jones, and Gene Richards would be around with lots of little tidbits to offer if you could get them talking.

Bobby Tolan called me one night and told me to come to the park early the next day. He handed me a fungo bat, one of those long, light, skinny bats coaches use for hitting fly balls to outfielders. You wouldn't use a fungo in a game, it would break into pieces. Tolan said we were going to play soft toss. He put me in the batter's box, then crouched off the outside of the plate and lobbed balls underhand into the strike zone for me to hit.

He said to take a full swing like I was using my bat.

I was shocked to see how far I was hitting the ball, and the kind of bat speed I was generating with this fungo. The fungo is a cheater, very light, so it showed me what was possible. I began to understand that in order to swing a wood bat and swing it right, the key to everything is bat speed.

I began to notice what I was doing at the plate. In college, many times I'd hit a ball and come back to the dugout and somebody would ask me what kind of pitch I hit. I didn't know. In Walla Walla, I started paying a little more attention. Fungo drills woke me up to the kind of bat speed I could have if I really worked at it.

TROPHIES

My most memorable hit in sixteen years was in the 1996 season. We were coming down the stretch trying to get into the playoffs and were neck-in-neck with the Dodgers. It was a Saturday game, score tied 2-2, bases loaded, eighth inning, and I'm up. If we win the game, we're in the playoffs.

They brought in Mark Guthrie, a lefthander, to pitch to me. He got ahead in the count, 0 and two. I got a base hit, in what I call my patented 5.5 hole, which is the hole between short and third. Two runs scored. We won the game. We made the playoffs. For me that's the biggest hit I've had as a professional. The pressure was on, and I delivered.

My biggest hit before that was in the playoffs in 1984. We were tied 3-3 in the fifth and final game. Runners on first and second, one out. Rick Sutcliffe was pitching. That was the year he won the Cy Young Award. He was dominant, but he started to run out of gas that game. I hit a rocket right at Ryne Sandberg. It took a bad hop over his head and went into the gap for a double. It gave us the lead in the last game of the playoffs, and got us to the World Series.

Besides hitting, the biggest thing I've ever done as a ballplayer was win my first Gold Glove. That will always be a great moment. The reason is that I had to work so hard at becoming a good outfielder. When I first came up, I had no arm strength, and I was inaccurate to boot. And when I arrived on the scene there were guys like Dave Parker and André Dawson out there. They were the best. Becoming a good outfielder was no easy deal for Old Blub. Winning that first Gold Glove was the best individual thing I've ever done.

AWARDS

(THROUGH 1997 SEASON)

NL BATTING TITLES (8)

Year	Avg
1984	.351*
1987	.370*
1988	.313
1989	.336
1994	.394*
1995	.368*
1996	.353
1997	.372*

(*led majors)

ALL-STAR TEAM (13)
1984, 1985*, 1986*, 1987*, 1989*, 1990, 1991*, 1992*, 1993, 1994*, 1995*, 1996*, 1997*

(*voted to start by fans)

SPORTING NEWS ALL-STAR TEAM (5)
1984, 1986, 1987, 1988, 1989

PADRES MOST VALUABLE PLAYER (7)
(as voted by San Diego chapter of BBWAA) 1984, 1986, 1987, 1988, 1994, 1995, 1997

RAWLING'S GOLD GLOVE AWARD (5)
1986, 1987, 1989, 1990, 1991

SPORTING NEWS SILVER SLUGGER TEAM (7)
1984, 1986, 1987, 1989, 1994, 1995, 1997

BRANCH RICKEY AWARD
(top community activist in Major League Baseball) 1995

NL PLAYER OF THE MONTH (5)
April 1984
June 1987
July 1988
August 1993
May 1997

MOORES AWARD
(Padre who most exemplifies community spirit of John and Becky Moores) 1995

MOST CARING ATHLETE
As named in USA Today Weekend Magazine 1997

The fungo drill with Tolan also made Gwynn start thinking about bats. First he bought himself a fungo just so he could swing it whenever he wanted and feel the speed. Then he began reconsidering the bat he was using. In minor league organizations like Walla Walla, they order bats wholesale. Players don't have the luxury of specialized bats as they do in the majors. Gwynn was swinging a 34-inch, 32-ounce bat, and he realized that he couldn't handle it as well as the smaller bat he had used in college. It wasn't aluminum, a bat that makes hitting easier, and it was too big.

I was hitting some home runs, but it wasn't the way I wanted to do it. It didn't feel right. About three weeks into our Short-A season we were in Eugene, Oregon. We'd just gotten paid. We weren't making that much back then, maybe $600 a month. I took the last $40 I had and bought two wood bats, Mike Ivy model 0-16.

The bats were 32 inches, 31 ounces. I had been hitting the ball pretty good, but after I bought these two bats I went on a tear. I must have led off three or four games in a row with home runs. I learned a valuable lesson: when you come to pro-

fessional baseball you pretty much have to take what they give you unless you're willing to pay for your own stuff. I was smart enough to realize that if I invested in a couple of bats it could pay dividends later on. And it did. For the next two weeks I was on fire.

After watching Gwynn hit a League-leading .331 in his first six weeks in Walla Walla, the Padres organization sent him to Amarillo, a Double-A team. They say if you can hit AA pitching, you can hit in the big leagues. Gwynn finished the season with a .462 average. After that, he says, there were no more surprises.

I arrived in Amarillo as a hot prospect, leading the North-West League in hitting. I had my little bat, and I had been ripping the ball. My first at-bat in Amarillo was a five-hopper to second base. The guy threw me out easy. I came back to the bench disgusted. I was bitching about hitting a five-hopper, and the guys said fine, get a hit next time. And I did. I got a double. Then another one. I ended up going three-for-four and all of a sudden I was winning these guys over. They started to see that all that hype was legit, I guess.

Gwynn went to Padres spring training camp the following year. He was confi-

dent about hitting. But he worried about his throwing arm, and he wasn't great on the base paths. He listened to the vets and tried to become more rounded.

He started the 1982 season in what is called the "instructional," or AAA, league, considered an accurate barometer of a player's potential. Gwynn hit .328 in 93 games with the Hawaiian Islanders of the Pacific Coast AAA League before being summoned by the San Diego Padres. He'd been in the minors a grand total of one year. His cumulative numbers from college through the minor leagues: a batting average of .390 with 34 home runs.

His first major league appearance was in San Diego against the Philadelphia Phillies, July 19, 1982.

I was excited, but I wouldn't say I was nervous—except about my parents being in the stands. The crowd was buzzing because I was a hometown guy who made it. My first time at bat I got a standing ovation. They knew me from my San Diego State days. My minor league stats

STEVE CARLTON. "I NEVER FELT I WAS A GOOD HITTER UNTIL I GOT A HIT OFF STEVE. HE COULD REALLY HIDE THE BALL."

flashed on the score board.

First time up I hit a sacrifice fly and drove in a run to put us ahead, temporarily. My second at-bat I lined out. I was hitting the ball good, but you don't want to go two or three games before you get your first major league hit. Third time up I lined the ball into left center for a double. Sid Monge was the pitcher. That was nice because Monge was a lefthander, one of those lefties that is particularly tough on left-handed hitters like me.

Pete Rose was playing first base for the Phillies, and he backed up the play. As I pulled up at second the scoreboard lit up: TONY GWYNN'S FIRST MAJOR LEAGUE HIT! Rose saw it and walked over. "That's your first major league hit?" I said, "Yeah." He said, "Well congratulations. Just don't try to catch me in one night."

Pete Rose had always been a hero of mine. I loved the way he played the game. It was one of those moments that will always mean a lot to me.

The next night Steve Carlton was pitching, and he abused me, fooled me completely. I said if it took the rest of my career, I would hit a hard one off him. It took four years. He went from the

Phillies to the Twins to the Giants before he returned to the Phillies. In 1986, I finally got a hit off him, a grounder up the middle.

That first season I hit .289, which was pretty good. But I didn't hit lefties very well and I also had to learn to pull the ball, so I played winter ball. I slipped rounding first and landed on my hand, broke my wrist. I was out until July of the 1983 season. My first game back I went three-for-four, then I went into a slump for a month. That's when I began taping my at-bats. The first time I saw myself swing I knew immediately what I was doing wrong. Coaches were telling me stuff, but when I saw myself it made all the difference. I went on a 25-game hitting streak and hit .360 the rest of the year. Video became a big part of my career.

PETE ROSE. "CHARLIE HUSTLE. THIS IS HOW I ALWAYS THINK OF PETE, SLIDING HEAD FIRST WITH DIRT FLYING."

STEALING

Stealing bases was something I had to learn to do when I came up to the Majors. I had to learn how to read pitchers, look for habits and tendencies. Greg Riddock, our first base coach, taught me a lot about base stealing.

I'd been using video to study hitting for years, but we never thought to use video for pitchers so we could get their moves. The year I started doing that I stole 56 bases. Nobody believed I could steal 56 bases.

I was caught 12 times; 56 of 68. Pretty good. Today, I can't steal bases like I used to but I'm still pretty smart on base. I still can read pitchers pretty well. If I get a jump, I'll go. I stole in double digits the last couple of years.

You have to take the opportunity to steal when you can, but I just can't go out there running around and sliding in a carefree way. The way my knees are, I have to save myself a little bit. But running the bases provides some of the best excitement in baseball. Lots of times I get over to first or second and they don't pay any attention to me. I'm not supposed to be stealing bases. But if you give me a chance, I'll take it.

OPPOSITE: GWYNN SCORES THE WINNING RUN (FROM FIRST) IN THE 10TH INNING OF THE 1994 ALL-STAR GAME AT PITTSBURGH. FOLLOWING PAGES: GWYNN TAKES A BREAK IN RIGHT FIELD DURING A PITCHING CHANGE.

Hitting Clinic

IRST COMES THE BAT. I use a short bat because I feel I can control it better. The Louisville Slugger I use now is 33 inches long and weighs 30.5 ounces. I like a thicker handle because I broke a finger once, and it doesn't close all the way. My bat has what they call a "Gwynn finish": the barrel is painted black, but the handle is just sanded, unpainted ash for a better grip. I can rub pine tar and resin into it. Pine tar and resin are the smell of baseball.

I don't feel intimidated because my teammates use 34- or 35-inch bats. I have to use what works for me. Rule number one: Get a bat that feels comfortable in your hands.

Rule number two: Get yourself a good pair of batting gloves. They should fit snug, with no wrinkles. I use tape on the fingers of my gloves because I have skinny fingers. The smallest glove Franklin makes is still too loose, so I tape the fingers to keep them snug. You don't want wrinkles because you'll get blisters, and it's tough enough to hit with two good hands.

Now you're ready to go to work.

THE GRIP

It's amazing to me how many people don't hold the bat right. Just as in tennis or golf, the right grip is important. The bat should actually lay in your fingers.

A lot of hitters think they have to anchor the bat in the palm of the bottom hand. I don't recommend that. As you start to understand why you do what you do, you will find that having the bat lay across your fingers will give you a lot more control. It will give you a better feel for when you're doing things right. If you have the bat stuck in your palm, you just don't get the same feel for what you're doing.

I can generate a lot more bat speed when the bat is in my fingers. Using the

fingers of your top hand to hold the bat correctly is even more important. The bat must lay gently across the fingers of your top hand because that allows the bottom hand to dominate.

Ted Williams and I have debated this point. For me, the bottom hand is the dominant hand because it pulls the bat through the zone. The top hand is the guide. As you pull that bat through the zone, you don't want the top hand trying to take over. You want it to play backup, guiding the bat through the zone.

Ted thinks differently. Ted was a dead pull hitter, so for him, a different grip made sense. As he started to swing—and he was more of an upright guy, with his back elbow up—he'd get about a foot into his swing from the hitting position and the top hand would take over. And he would pull the ball. Fielders would shift over on him, and he'd still pull. They'd pitch him outside and still he'd pull the ball, and he was able to hit .400, which tells you what kind of a hitter Williams was.

But I believe that the bottom hand is the dominant hand in today's game. Take a look at your videotapes to see where the good hitters hit the ball. They use the

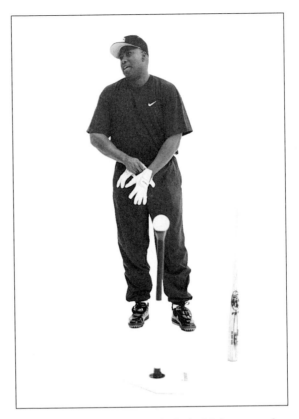

whole field, from the left field line to the right field line. And they do it with authority, with some drive, with some backspin. That indicates the bottom hand has to be the dominant hand, pulling the bat through the zone while the top hand is just guiding the barrel.

In order for that to work, you can't squeeze the bat with your top hand in a death grip. If you choke the bat with the top hand, as you come through the zone, in the course of the swing, you will get to the point where the bottom hand can't lead anymore. The top hand

STAN MUSIAL'S
STANCE (TOP LEFT)
WAS CLASSIC. CAL
RIPKEN (TOP RIGHT)
KEEPS CHANGING.
WILLIE MAYS (LEFT)
GETS TO THE HITTING
POSITION.

will take over, and the bat will roll over. It has to.

But if you lay the bat gently across your top hand, the bottom hand will pull the bat as far as it will go: through the hitting zone, through the contact point, across home plate, through the ball, and you'll get way out front into your follow-through before the bat begins to roll over. And at that point, it doesn't matter. That's why it's important that the top hand is loosey goosey.

THE STANCE

Once you're at the plate, it doesn't matter where you stand. Front of the box, back of the box; in on the plate, or out. Find a spot where you're comfortable and stay there. When I get to the plate, I split it front to back. My feet are spread about shoulder width so I can be balanced. You've got to have good balance and I want my weight right in the middle. You'll see Freddie McGriff or George Brett leaning on that back leg. That's fine, too. Whatever you think works.

Now you're at the plate. What do you do while you're waiting for the pitcher to finish messing around—pulling at his cap, spitting, grabbing the resin bag,

hitching up his pants and looking at the ducks flying past—before he finally delivers the ball? You get in your stance. The stance is anything that passes the time and gets the batter prepared to hit between the pre-pre-windup and the delivery of the ball.

GARY SHEFFIELD READY TO PULL THE TRIGGER.

If you look at all the good hitters, what's important is not so much where the bat starts in the stance, it's what position it's in the moment before it starts to come forward. All good hitters use their own stances. The key thing is when that front foot comes down and touches the ground, the bat should be in a cocked position. So it's not how you start, it's what position the barrel head is in and what position your body is in when that front foot hits the ground.

Some guys start early, some guys start late. But once the front foot hits the ground you want that bat to be in a position where all you have left is to take the knob of the bat to the ball. This means you want to start your hands where they don't have that far to go to get to the hitting position. I base that on what I've seen other good hitters do.

Stan Musial used to stand in with his bat straight up and down. Ted Williams was a straight-up-and-down guy. Willy Mays moved his hands around a lot. Hank Aaron did too. So did Reggie Jackson. Cal Ripken has had three different stances in three years. Now he just holds the bat still

HANK AARON. "ONE OF THE ALL-TIME GREATEST."

on his shoulder, just touching his shoulder. Even a guy with a lot of different stances, Chuck Carr of the Astros, Mr. Hot Dog Man, gets to the hitting position. When every good hitter's front foot hits the ground, his hands and bat come to the cocked position and the least amount of movement you make to get to that position is best.

Then there's back elbow choice: up, or down. I'm a flat elbow guy. My back elbow stays pretty relaxed. It's easier for me, but half the guys will be hitting with it up, the other half will have it down.

I believe in keeping my stance simple, but it's just like any other facet of hitting: if you put six different guys together talking about hitting, you're going to get six theories. But when it comes to that moment when you pull the trigger, only the terminology will be different.

Of course a big part of the stance, and all the stylin' going on in the batter's box during the pre-windup and the pre-pre-windup, is just a lot of posturing. What's happening between the pitcher and the batter is a battle of coolness. The pitcher is going through all his body language to let the batter know he's tough, he's in charge, he's gonna get him. And by wiggling

around and brandishing his club, the batter is delivering his message: I'm the man, and you're dead meat, pal, because I'm gonna line one of your pitches on a rope for extra bases.

When you walk up to the plate, the best place for that kind of resolve is in your head. You've got to be confident, even cocky. Because the pitcher's job is to get your timing off, you can't let yourself or him think he's going to be successful.

When I get up to face Randy Johnson, thinking that I'm the man is not easy. He's 6'11" and he's throwing 99 miles an hour. With his long body and arms, his delivery seems to be coming from right field, behind my right shoulder. But in my own mind, I'm the man. It might not work out that way, but when I get up there, I know—I'm going to hit the ball.

STEP SOFTLY

You're in the batter's box, in your stance, and the pitcher gets ready to let the ball go. When he gets to his release point, the action should be like this: you take your stride, stepping softly on the ball of your front foot. At the same time, your hands have reached the hitting, or cocked, position. In the hitting position, the top hand is right by your ear. It's almost in that spot where coaches will warn you to watch out. You do not want to go past that point because the bat will get wrapped around your head.

But in order to be a good hitter, sooner or later you must get your hands to the cocked position as you land softly on the ball of the front foot. That's the first part.

During the whole hitting process, you must maintain balance. When I get up to the plate, I like my weight to be centered. I like to have it split 50-50 on both feet, or maybe 45-55 with the back foot a little heavier. This way, when I take my stride and put my hands back in the hitting position there won't be any weight transfer.

Balance means being in a good, comfortable position at the plate. That allows me to wait on the pitch. For me, the longer I can wait, the better hitter I am. Every pitch is not going to be a fastball. They're going to slip in a curve, or a forkball, or a slider. In order to hit those pitches, you have to be in a balanced position at the plate.

When I take my stride there shouldn't be any actual body movement. When I stride, I don't go forward. The front leg is on its own, and I want it to land softly. The softer I am on the front foot, the less movement I'm going to have and the easier it will be to stay back. A coach once told me the way I put that front foot down wouldn't kill any ants, and that's how I like it.

I learned from making mistakes. When I first started out in the Big Leagues, I tried to get the swing going real quick, and what I found out was that the harder I landed with the front foot, the easier it was to lose my balance. When I started breaking down my swing, when I used video for the first time, I saw that any time I snapped that foot down, my balance was gone.

As hitters, sometimes we feel out of sync. The reason usually is that as we stride we allow ourselves to move forward. And if your upper body goes forward—if your shoulders go forward and your head goes forward—then you might

KEVIN BROWN APPROACHING THE RELEASE POINT.

you'll be surprised how long you actually have to wait for that ball to come to you.

RELEASE POINT

When does all this activity happen, this split-second flow of landing softly on the front foot with the hands cocked in the hitting position, all with good balance? For me, it's when the pitcher gets to his release point. Then it's just about seeing the baseball, determining where it's going to go and where my barrel's got to be to meet it. And I should be able to hit it. If it's in the zone—my hitting zone, not necessarily the strike zone—I should be able to hit it.

When the pitcher gets to his release point, it's important for you to be relaxed and comfortable as well as balanced. That will give you more time to decipher what the pitch is once the ball leaves the pitcher's hand. Some pitchers tip off the pitch by showing their fingers when they throw it. If it's a curve ball, you only see half the ball—and the hand might be angled. For a fast ball, the fingers are usually straight up. Greg Maddox's change-up you don't see at all. But the more balanced and relaxed you are, the more time you'll have to figure it all out.

as well pack it in and wait until the next inning because you're out. The quicker you understand the balance factor, the more successful you'll be.

The sequence I've described—the cocked hands, the stride, the front foot down softly while maintaining balance—happens in a split second. There's no stop, no hesitation. It's a sequential flow based on timing. And it's all going on in that split second when you are deciding whether to swing, or take the pitch.

If you can do all of that right, then

You've got to be paying attention, concentrating. You can't expect to go up to the plate and be successful if you are not focused. When I get up to the batter's box I focus in on a spot, which is usually the pitcher's cap. Not the top of his cap, but the team logo on his cap. Once he starts his windup and comes into his stretch, there's going to be a slow shift of my eyes to wherever his release point is going to be. I don't really want to spend a lot of time looking around while I'm in the batter's box.

Exactly when you lift your foot and take your stride varies, depending on the kind of pitcher you're facing. If it's a Tom Candeotti, who throws a real slow knuckle ball, it doesn't make any sense to sit up there and start going into your routine when he gets to the release point because the ball isn't coming to you for a while. But with pitchers like John Smoltz or Randy Johnson, guys who throw real

GREG MADDOX, THE MASTER OF LOCATION.

hard, maybe you start just a hair before they get to the release point. It depends on the type of guy on the mound.

Ball movement is the thing in my league. A guy like Gregg Maddox isn't the most overpowering or intimidating guy, but he has great movement and great location. He puts the ball where he wants it. For a hitter, that's just as hard as facing a guy throwing 97 miles an hour. It's not that difficult to put your bat on a fast ball, but it's very difficult to put a real good swing on the ball of a location pitcher. If he's got good ball movement he's got a great chance of keeping the hitter off balance and win a lot of ball games.

| THE SWING |

The swing makes the most sense to me when I think of taking the knob of the bat to the ball. Or, if you prefer, taking the bottom hand right to the ball. But for me, it's the knob of the bat.

In Williams' book, *The Science of Hitting*, there are photographs of other great hitters. One of them is of Hank Aaron at the plate, shot from centerfield. Aaron is in mid-swing, and all you can see in the picture is the knob of the bat with Aaron's hands wrapped around the handle. The

rest of the bat is hidden because it is straight out behind the knob. It's just an awesome shot. That picture really impressed me and started my thinking about bringing the knob of the bat to the ball. Bring the knob, and the barrel will naturally follow. You'd think there was no way the barrel could catch up, but it does, every time.

So you take the knob back and then take the bottom hand—which is your left hand if you're right-handed; your right hand if you're left-handed—right to the

OPPOSITE: **FRANK THOMAS.**

JOHN SMOLTZ. "BY THIS POINT, YOU SHOULD HAVE DECIDED WHETHER OR NOT TO SWING AT THE PITCH."

ball. You'll be surprised how much bat speed you can generate by letting the knob lead the way. The barrel head is not far behind, and it comes from the hitting zone because it's following the knob. It must!

The object is to hit the ball hard. Sometimes as hitters we set our goals too high. Anyone who's ever played the game of baseball can attest to that. Every time we go to the plate, we want to get a hit. We don't care what kind of hit it is, we just want a hit. But a better goal is to go to the plate and see how many times we can do things correctly and hit the ball hard. Because if you hit the ball hard, the chances of somebody out there making a play are going to be a lot less than if you hit it slow. The harder you hit the ball, the tougher it is for the defense. And the more times you get to that balanced position, step softly on the ball of your front foot, get your hands to the hitting position, and take the knob of the bat to the ball, the more times you're going to hit the ball hard.

One more thing: A lot of hitters change their swing when they get behind in the count. When they get two strikes on them, they choke up on the bat and shorten their swing—they're just going to try to meet the ball. I say, why? Take your swing, the same swing every time. If you know why you do what you do, why change it? Why shorten up? Why panic? Why give control to the pitcher?

As a hitter, I have to know I will get my bat on the ball. I take my same swing every time. I struck out 28 times in 1997, and that's a lot for me. But that means I put the bat on the ball more than 600 times. So if I have two strikes on me, that isn't going to change anything. I've still got one more opportunity to hit the ball. Therefore I'm going up there and do things the way I want to do them.

The object is not to hit the baseball, it's to hit *through* the baseball. Should you let the bat go with the top hand at the end of your swing? That's your choice. Sometimes I let the top hand go and

sometimes I don't. There's nothing in this that's going to make you a better hitter. A lot of hitters feel they get through the ball a lot better after making contact by letting go with that top hand.

When I swing inside-out on a ball in-side, I try to get my top hand out of the way. After I make contact I just let it go because I know my top arm can't take the crunch. That's one of your choices. You can do the helicopter or not, where the bat held only in the bottom hand does almost a full circle over your head at the end of the swing. But to let go or not isn't too important.

It's the same as the old adage that says the back foot must stay on the ground. I refer you to Frank Thomas, who proves every year that the back foot definitely does not have to stay on the ground. Thomas hits 35 homers and drives in 100 runs a year while lifting his back foot. Either you can make these things work, or you can't. The object of this whole drill is to hit the ball hard, so letting the top hand go, or lifting the back foot—these are things you're going to have to experiment with as you work.

KNOW YOURSELF

The best way to come to terms with these choices is to know yourself. The good hitters develop an understanding of why they do what they do. Once that understanding is reached, they can make well-considered, productive choices. Knowing yourself is one of the biggest reasons that things work.

For instance, weight training is very important for me because I need very strong legs to do what I do. I don't look like your typical athlete. I'm not 6'3", 185 pounds, and I don't run like a deer. I'm a little chunky guy, but I make it work and I'm proud of that. I shouldn't be able to do any of this stuff I'm doing—but the reason I'm still around, the reason I make it work, is that I know myself.

Another example: The reason I use a short bat is because I know it's what I need to do the job. I don't have the upper body strength to swing a big heavy club, so I don't try to use one.

Every good hitter should not only know himself, he should know his team-mates and try to help them. Baseball is about winning, and the best way to win is to help everybody on the team that you can. But you've got to be able to accept the help. When a guy is struggling, he gets suggestions from the head coach and from this guy and that guy, and if he doesn't know himself he's going to be confused. But if you know what it is you have to do to stop struggling, then the

advice can be helpful. Knowing yourself isn't your coach's responsibility, it's your responsibility.

SECRET WEAPON

There are a lot of expensive machines on the market to help you become a better hitter. I've got most of them because the manufacturers send them to me to try out. Some of them aren't bad. But I know about a little device you can buy for about $15 that will help you learn a lot about hitting. It's called a batting tee. Then buy, for 50¢ apiece, some little items called whiffle balls. The combination of batting tee and whiffle ball is the best thing ever invented to learn about hitting. The tee and whiffle ball will let you know if you're doing things correctly.

The tee is not home plate. The tee is the hitting area. That means you can move the tee around to wherever you want. Whatever you happen to be working on, you can move it there. If I wanted to work on the ball inside, I would park the tee so the ball was set up on the inside of the plate. If I wanted to work on the ball away, I'd kick the tee out a little bit.

If you are working on a ball down the middle, or a ball on the inside that you want to pull, and you hit the whiffle ball correctly, you should hear air whooshing through the holes as it flies through the air, not that whinier spinning sound. If you hit it incorrectly, underneath for instance, it will have backspin. If you hit it on top, it will have top spin. If you take your hands too quick inside the ball, it'll have inside out spin. If you go around the ball, it'll spin outside in. The spin will let you know if you're swinging correctly, or

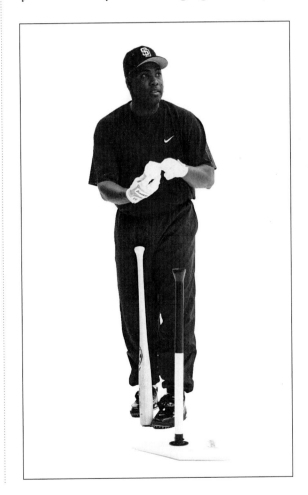

what you're doing wrong. If you are working on trying to hit a ball inside to the opposite field, and you do it correctly, then the whiffle ball should spin inside-out, or sometimes it will have top spin. All it takes is several whiffle balls and a couple of swings. When you hit it right, most of the time it comes off the tee as a knuckle ball.

I try to keep this game simple. As a player I haven't changed very much. But every year there's something that clicks and people ask me what I did that was different. Maybe I hit a few more home runs. I hit 17 homers in 1997. What did I do differently? Nothing. I'm doing the same thing I've been doing for the last 16 years, and I'm pretty much the same type of player I've always been. My approach, my work ethic, the things I do everyday haven't changed. When I suck, and I do at times, the batting tee and the whiffle ball get me back on track. They always have, and I'm certain they always will.

Hitting is not an exact science. When I go to the plate, sometimes I end up swinging, sometimes I'm slashing. Sometimes I'm just poking. Anybody can hit the heater up in the strike zone. But making

something happen is the key. If you can take what they give you and make something happen, that's a lot better.

I don't care what I look like at the plate. I just want to get it done. When there's a left-hander throwing a good slider away, sometimes you just can't reach it with a normal swing. You've got to slap and slash to get the barrel of the bat on the ball. There's nothing wrong with that if you can succeed.

I get a lot of credit as a hitter because I do whatever I have to do to put the ball in play. Sometimes it doesn't look like a beautiful, patented, heel-to-toe type of cut. It can be ugly, reaching out in front to get to the ball. But I have that ability. My hitting zone goes from three inches off my shoes to my neck if need be. I don't have to take the classic baseball swing; I can reach out in front and slap the ball for a hit. Or if I'm a little late, I can still put the barrel on the ball and haul it inside-out, down the third base line, with the pitcher cussing at me as I'm running to first.

No, hitting isn't a science. It's an art. That's why it's so satisfying, and so much fun.

THE ART

ROM THE TIME *he signed his first contract to play in the major leagues, Tony Gwynn became a dedicated student of baseball. To this day he's never stopped observing and asking questions about all aspects of the game. It's one of the remarkable things about him. One might expect that at age 37, with eight National League batting*

championships to his credit, Gwynn might be slipping quietly into the role of elder statesman, withdrawing a bit from the daily grind. But he often gets to the stadium early to view his videotapes, hang around the batting cage, and talk with other players. He asks questions and listens as much as he holds court—and it's always with a laugh, a smile, and a shrug—hey, all I know is what works for me.

GWYNN AND MERV RETTENMUND AT THE BATTING CAGE, DISCUSSING THE CRAFT OF HITTING.

It started in 1981 when Gwynn first signed with San Diego. On one of his first days in camp, Gwynn found himself in the same batting practice group as Broderick Perkins, the Padres' first baseman. After watching Perkins take his cuts, Gwynn asked him what he tried to accomplish in batting practice. Perkins said he liked to hit the ball the opposite way first—to left field if you're a left-handed hitter; to right field if you bat right-handed—because that's probably the hardest thing to do in baseball.

That was very interesting to me, because I hit the ball to the opposite field naturally. And Perkins said that's the hardest thing to do, to wait long enough on the pitch to be able to hit the ball to the opposite field; hitting a ball on the inside of the plate is easier because you just react.

I decided that day that I would make my living in baseball hitting the ball outside, and it's been my strength my whole career. I had to work on the ball inside. It took ten years and a lot of practice. But from that one conversation I started putting the pieces of the puzzle together. I figured out why I hit the ball to left field all the time: I wait until the last minute and practically take the ball out of the catcher's glove. I did it in Little League, I did it in high school, I did it in college, I did it when I first signed with the Padres, and I still do it.

If you ask most hitters which ball is easiest to hit, they're going to say the ball inside—the fast ball inside, the reaction pitch. So they go up there looking for it and, to me, that's a problem. If you are looking for the ball inside, you are going to have trouble adjusting to the ball outside. When I go up there, I'm thinking, outside. If the pitch is a ball inside, I'm going to trust that I can react and turn on

it. I can't look for the ball in and still hit the ball away, but I can commit to the ball away and hit the ball inside with the same swing. That's important: I don't swing any differently when the ball's inside.

There's an old axiom in baseball: until you can handle the ball away, you're not going to get the ball inside. For me it works the other way. I want the ball outside. I'd give a million dollars if I knew every pitch was going to be on the outside of the plate. But I'm not going to get it until I can handle the ball inside. In the Big Leagues, it's a game of adjustments, a constant cycle.

Former Padres' manager Dick Williams first got on me about learning to pull the ball and hit behind the runner, during the 1984 season. I was batting second in the lineup. Alan Wiggins was our lead-off man, and he was a speedster. He got on base. Gerry Royce was pitching for the Dodgers. I came up and hit a rocket right at the left fielder for an out.

Dick Williams didn't often get up and roam the dugout. If he had something to say to a guy, he'd have one of the coaches do it. But this time he walked over to me and said, "Tony, in that situation you gotta pull the f-ing ball." It stuck. Be-

cause I used to hit everything to the left side of second base.

Dick Williams is an interesting guy and playing for him was an experience. You were on pins and needles all the time, wondering when he would blow. But he taught me a lot about myself. If you made a mistake, he told you—and he didn't want excuses. "If you screwed up, say you screwed up," he would say. That has stayed with me to this day. I pay attention to little things because of Dick Williams.

IN THE ON-DECK CIRCLE, GWYNN GOES OVER HIS CHECKLIST, STUDIES PITCHER AND DEFENSE. "ONCE I'M IN THE CIRCLE, I CUT OFF COMMUNICATION. IT'S MY TIME." FOLLOWING PAGES: HITTING ONE UP THE MIDDLE AT QUALCOMM, THE PADRES' HOME BALLPARK.

Then Ted Williams got on my case about the inside pitch. He made his living from the middle of the plate in; I make my living from the middle of the plate out. Bob Costas put us together on the

GWYNN, OPPOSITE, AND WILLIAMS, ABOVE, TAKING CUTS. "MY HANDS ARE EXTENDED. HIS ARE CLOSE TO HIS BODY. THAT'S WHY HE HAD SO MUCH POWER."

spur of the moment on a radio show a couple years ago. The question was what to do with the ball inside. Williams spoke first, and then it was my turn. I was scared to death. Most people think Ted Williams was one of the three best hitters who ever played the game. He makes me feel inferior. I said I thought you just had to handle the ball inside, you didn't have to hit it out of the park.

At that, Ted Williams went off. He said the ball inside is the ball that major league history is made of. "You've got to turn on it. You've got to let it go." He said the only way to keep a pitcher honest is to hit that inside ball out of the park. That was the first time I ever spoke with Ted

Williams about hitting, and I assumed he was just defending the way he made his living. The problem is, if you just let your swing go, your chances of fouling the ball off or missing it are much greater. You've got to have a lot of confidence to just let it go.

But in the last several years I've tried to use my body to hit the inside pitch. I don't turn my hips. I do all the same things—get the front foot down softly, hands to the cocked position, bring the knob of the bat to the ball—but I let the swing go and use my natural quickness to hit the ball out in front of the plate. I can either wait on the inside pitch and hit flares to left, or let my swing go and hit it to right.

In 1996, I spoke with Ted Williams again. We must have gone on for an hour or so. This time I was more determined. I said, "Mr. Williams, with all due respect, I really think that if you just handle the pitch inside it will keep them honest." He said to me, "Son, you start hitting that inside ball out of the park and you'll see the difference. When you start hitting it out, they will not come inside."

Spring training in 1997 I sucked. I had worked all winter on hitting the inside pitch. I wanted to attack that ball, something I hadn't done very well before. If I struck out more, made more outs, no matter. I wanted to make them pay if they came inside.

None of it was working. I hit one home run in spring training. Most of my hits were singles. I was really questioning myelf. But when the season opened, here came Pete Harnish pitching the first game. I just knew what I was going to see: First time up, first pitch, sure enough, Harnish threw me a fastball. Base hit to left.

I was in sync most of the time in 1997 and my reactions were right. As the season went on, I thought, okay, if they come inside I'll be aggressive. I'm going to let it go. I had two home runs the first home stand. We went on the road and I hit two more home runs. I had four home runs ten games into the season. That never happened for me before. But that's what I wanted to do and I was able to do it. And because it was early in the season, the pitchers had to think differently when I came to the plate. I figured if I hit a few home runs early, I'd get the pitch that I really wanted, which was a fastball out over the plate, and I could go to left field

GWYNN GOING THROUGH HIS RITUAL OF DRAWING TWO LINES IN THE BATTER'S BOX FOR PRECISE FOOT LOCATION. ONE IS TOWARD THE PITCHER'S MOUND, THE OTHER IS PERPENDICULAR TO THE FIRST.

with it, because that's what I'd always done. To be a successful hitter you have to keep them honest, keep them guessing.

In the first half of the 1997 season they kept coming inside on me, as usual, and I hit 13 home runs. The second half of the season I only hit four home runs because I was getting the ball back outside where I like it. Since I've learned to hurt them with the inside pitch, they stay outside. So I have to tip my cap to Ted Williams. I didn't believe him for quite a while, but I have to say, he was absolutely right.

Ted Williams was so good at pulling the ball he could take the outside pitch and hit it like it was inside. Some guys can do that. Not me.

Some guys creep up and stand right on top of the plate. The ball that's outside is like down the middle to them, and the ball that's down the middle is like inside to them. On a ball inside, they have to decide if it's a ball or a strike, and then they have to learn how to keep it fair when they hit it. Barry Bonds is very good at that. There aren't many guys who can do that. Ken Griffey can do it, and Mark McGwire, too, but they're like me: not on top of the plate.

I stand off the plate, but I can reach the outside corner. I take my stride toward shortstop, so even with my short bat I can cover the outside of the plate without having to be on top of it. We all have different ways of getting the job done.

OPPOSITE: **RANDY JOHNSON DELIVERS. "IMAGINE BATTING LEFT AGAINST THIS GUY. IT'S NOT FUN TO FACE THE BIG UNIT. I'M READY TO DUCK RIGHT NOW."** RIGHT: **FERNANDO VALENZUELA.**

ONE-ON-ONE

There are some pitchers who are intimidating. I don't care how long you've been playing the game. When you have a guy like Randy Johnson on the mound throwing nearly 100 miles an hour from the same side you hit from, that can be a little intimidating.

I faced Randy Johnson a couple times in 1997. Once in spring training, and then in the All-Star game. But, if there are guys who intimidate you, it's best to keep it to yourself and go on about your business. Whether it's Randy Johnson or Joe Smith, the pitcher has to throw the ball over the plate, and the batter's job is to hit it.

I'm pragmatic about the intimidation game. When I'm over the plate, I doubt if I intimidate anybody. On the other hand, they've got to get me out. In my mind, if the ball goes over the plate, I'm going to hit it. I'm not going to strike out. If it goes over the plate, sooner or later I will hit it, and when I do connect, I expect to hit it hard. So the intimidation game doesn't have much of an effect on me now. But when I was younger, oh yeah!

The first time I saw Mario Soto I said

to myself, oh man, Mario Soto, 96 miles an hour, oh boy. Then you get up there, and you're thinking about that ball coming in at 96. . . . But you know, it's not that hard. It's going to get to the plate faster, that's all.

Never worry about what pitchers do. Make them worry about what you do. The first time I faced Tom Seaver or Steve Carlton or Fernando Valenzuela, I will admit, it was a little tense. Then there are the guys I admired when I was a kid: Don Sutton, Phil Niekro, Joe Niekro, Nolan Ryan, Mike Scott. There's an element of sand-lot fantasy about getting into the batter's box against a guy like that. All of a sudden I am being asked to come up and bust his chops.

LEFT TO RIGHT: **PHIL NEIKRO, JOE NEIKRO, MIKE SCOTT, TOM SEAVER, MARIO SOTO, DANNY NEAGLE.**

But once you get past that, there is no one who can intimidate you. There will be some guys who you don't hit very well, but intimidation isn't a factor.

I look forward to facing the guys I don't hit well because I know sooner or later it's got to turn. There are a few, like Danny Neagle, who own me. I'm 3 for 27 against Neagle. But one reason I love the game of baseball is that sooner or later I will hit him. And when that table starts to turn, he will not be a happy camper.

During the home stretch in 1997, we were playing the Braves. Bruce Bochy, our manager, wanted me to take a day off because Neagle was pitching. I said, no way, I'm not taking Neagle-day off, I'm facing him. Bochy reminded me I was 3

for 24 against him, but I refused to take a day off. So I went out there and took my licks, 0 for 3 with a walk. I didn't get the ball out of the infield all night long.

I don't see Neagle's ball. I don't see it out of his hand, I can't find his release point, and I don't know why. There are other guys who give me problems. Tony Foss with the Cardinals. I don't see the ball out of his hand either. Then there's Omar Olivarez, who I'm hitting at a 1-for-20 clip. He's got pretty decent stuff, but it's nothing unusual. Just down-in-the-strike-zone kind of stuff that I should be hitting. Sooner or later it will turn.

I study my at-bats against Neagle on video because I can't figure out why I don't see the ball. We're not talking about

a guy who's throwing 95 miles per hour. Neagle's best fastball might get up to 91–92. For the most part he's serving up breaking balls or change-ups. But he has movement, inside-outside, up and down. He gets hitters off balance, and he gets

them out. He'll never strike out everybody, but he's good at keeping you off balance enough so that you can't go up there and sit on certain pitches.

The toughest guy I ever hit against was Nolan Ryan. When he was on, man,

forget about it. He was throwing three pitches, throwing them all for strikes, and all three of those pitches were better than anybody else's. When he was throwing his fastball well, nobody threw it harder. When he threw his curve ball well, nobody had more break. And when he threw his changeup well, nobody had as much movement on the ball. And all of those pitches were well disguised.

Ryan has punched me out more than anybody, I'm sure, but I still loved the challenge of getting up against him. Even in his mid-forties, he could pump his heater in at 98, 99. The interesting thing is that I began to get comfortable hitting against him because I'd faced him so many times. And when you get comfortable, you don't worry so much about the 98–99-mile-per-hour heater because you know you can hit it.

I was completely intimidated by Nolan Ryan early on. I didn't want to piss him off. I just wanted to go up to the plate and try to hit the ball. As I faced him more and more, I began to realize things,

LEFT: KNUCKLE BALLER TOM CANDIOTTI. OPPOSITE: NOLAN RYAN. HIS PITCHES WERE WELL-DISGUISED.

pick up habits. If he threw me one fast-ball, the rest would be breaking balls and change-ups. When he started throwing that change-up, I started sitting on it and getting base hits off of him. But he struck me out more than anybody. Lifetime I would guess I'm right around .280, .290 against Ryan. And that's respectable, I guess. But he was in that "hate-to-face" category for a long time.

John Candelaria, a nasty left-hander, is also in that category. I never could take a really good swing off Candelaria. But I'd rather face these guys than duck them. You'll never turn it around unless you get up there and try to hit against people like Candelaria. Last season I hit a two-run homer off of him my first time at bat. I was cranked. Yeah! I got him! This thing's gonna turn around now. Then I went 0 for 6 against him.

Fernando Valenzuela was really good in his heyday. His habit of staring at the sky in mid-delivery was odd. But when you have 80 at-bats against Valenzuela lifetime, you get over that kind of stuff. It's like Hideo Nomo now, with the funky wind-up. Nobody knew how to really attack him because we'd never seen anything like that before and he was able to

take advantage of hitters. But now, three years in, hitters are starting to bust Nomo a little bit. He can't understand why, after the success he had early. But that's the big leagues. You might have success early in your career, but you've got to keep digging deep in the barrel to prove you can do it again and again.

Don Sutton was a lot of fun to hit against. He was very much like Greg Maddox is today. Sutton wasn't overpowering, but he had four really good pitches that he could throw any time. He was tough. I faced him in a spring training game and the first time up I doubled. I hit a fastball away inside-out, right down the left field line. The next time up I doubled down the right field line. He threw a fastball inside that I was able to turn on. After I got to second base, Sutton just turned and looked at me and shook his head. "You're unbelievable," he said.

It's little things like that I always remember because Don Sutton was one of my favorite pitchers to watch when I was a kid. He played with the Dodgers, the team I rooted for. I'm really pleased he made the Hall of Fame. Guys like Sutton had a big influence on my career because they went about their business the way it should be done. Every fourth or fifth day you could count on Don Sutton to go out there and give you seven innings, pitch a real good game, keep his team in the ballgame.

The game has changed. More than once during the course of a game I have faced five different pitchers: the starter, the long man, the middle man, the set-up man, and the closer. More than at any

tate the action. It makes it a little bit easier for me to face five different guys in a night because I'm letting them take the lead. I'll take what they give me and try to do something with it. They do something and I counter.

When I think of closers, Dennis Eckersley always comes to mind. He's still good. He doesn't have the pop in his fastball that he had early in his career,

LEFT TO RIGHT: **HIDEO NOMO, DON SUTTON, DICK WILLIAMS.**

other time in the history of baseball you really have to know yourself, because it's a big challenge facing so many different pitchers.

I've always liked to let the pitcher dic-

but he's still got a lot of guts. He can still get you out. He got me out in the playoffs in 1996. I came up with a man on second, two outs, the Cardinals were up by a run. I hit a ball that was going right up the middle, through his legs for a base hit, and he came up with it. After the play he did that thing that he does, cocking his fist and yelling. He's done that his whole career. I didn't say anything, but I thought to myself, if I ever get a chance to return the favor, I'll do the same thing.

And I did. In 1997, we were playing the Cardinals in San Diego. Eckersley came in to close. They were up by two and we had runners on first and second, two outs. I hit a ball into the left center field gap that scored two runs to tie the ballgame. After he got the ball and was walking out to the mound, I didn't look at him, but I shook my fist and gave him one of his own yells—*Yeeaahhh!*

I don't know if that's considered right or wrong, but when he got me out I didn't say anything. And the next time, I won the battle, drove in the runs, tied the game. So I gave it back. That's baseball.

OUCH!

I hate getting hit. We all hate getting hit. But every batter has to deal with it. The fear of getting hit is what the pitcher's intimidation card is all about, because when your body gets hit with a 4-ounce ball traveling 90 or 100 miles an hour, it's going to smart. You can't give in to that and still get your job done.

I don't get hit much. I don't know why.

But when I do get hit by a pitch I remember it. One night we played the Dodgers and Scott Radinsky came out of the bull pen. We had a man on second, one out, and Radinsky's got left handers coming up back to back, Steve Finley and myself. The first pitch he threw really jammed Finley, but somehow he fought it off and hit a broken bat flare just inside the bag at third. It went down the line for a double and knocked in a run. The Dodgers were trying to win the division, and now they're bumming.

Radinsky was upset: he threw a good pitch, and Finley got lucky and doubled down the line. It was bogus. Now I come up to the plate and we're in the same situation. Man on second, one out. The score is 3 to 1, Padres.

I know Radinsky is mad because he's walking around the mound and looking daggers at Finley. So I step up and he's on the rubber, just rubbing his foot side to side. He does this about ten times. So I step out and then get back in, and I thought to myself, he isn't going to hit me is he? And sure enough, first pitch—

DENNIS ECKERSLEY DOING HIS PATENTED YELL AFTER GETTING THE JOB DONE.

SCOTT RADINSKY.

pow!—hits me right on the elbow.

Now I'm pissed. While I understood Radinsky being upset, I'm the wrong guy to throw at. On my way to first I took my helmet off, looked at him and said, "I hope you're happy now, Scott. The prob lem is, it doesn't take away that double Finley hit off that great pitch. What are you hitting me for?"

Radinsky just looked at me. When I get to first, the coach usually comes over and says something, but he stayed away. He knew I was steaming.

That's one of those rare moments in this game where you just put a check mark by a guy's name. I don't do it very often, but I've got a check mark by Radinsky's name now, because I know he hit me on purpose. From here on out, if he's on the hill, I'm going to try like hell to hit the ball right back through the box and let him know how it feels.

I can charge the mound and get into a fight, get fined, suspended, but that's not healthy for me and it's not healthy for my ball club. So the next time I'm going back up the box.

Curt Schilling hit me on purpose three years ago and to this day he denies it. I said, "Okay, you can deny it, but next time I'm going right back through the box." It's one of those games you play with yourself. They know my bat control is pretty good, so if I say I intend to do it, they might think I can.

Most of the time, I let the pitchers dic tate the action. But every now and then the situation comes up where I can turn it around. After Radinsky hit me I told the press, "I know he hit me on purpose, and so from now on, he better keep his stuff way in or way out because I'm going right back up the box."

The next time I face him, I don't have to worry about where the ball's going to be. It's going to be well off the plate or way inside. Either way, he's going to have hell to pay. You don't get that opportunity very often. So when you do, take advantage of it, make the best of it.

Always stir the pot. "I'm gonna get him. He's gonna lay a ball out over the plate, and it's going right back up the middle and take his hat off."

Getting hit by a pitch hurts. A lot of guys steel themselves against it and don't even give the pitcher a reaction. I don't buy that myself, because if it hurts me I'm going down. I'm not going to sit there and start crying, but I'm going to tell you if it hurts.

There are unwritten rules in the game of baseball. Sometimes when they throw at a guy like me on purpose, people want retribution right away. I never say anything. I take care of my own business my own way. But the manager might feel differently. After Radinsky nailed me, Todd Zeile came up in the Dodger's half of the

CURT SCHILLING.

inning, and our pitcher threw one behind him, right behind his legs. He didn't get hit, but the message was delivered.

Sometimes it's just an accident. In 1995, I got hit by a pitcher with the Pirates. He had me 0-2. He just wanted to come inside with a fastball, get me off the plate so he could go away with a breaking ball. But he lost it and the ball kicked me right on the elbow. I went down like I was shot. After the initial shock of it, you get back up and keep on. My elbow blew up like a balloon.

Some guys wear an elbow pad, but I can't. Maybe I would if I got hit there enough, but I don't crowd the plate. The pitchers have to keep those guys crowding the plate honest, so they throw inside, and the plate crowders get hit a lot. That's why they wear elbow pads. I don't know if a pad would interrupt my swing, but it feels uncomfortable.

I don't even like shin pads. You foul balls off your foot so often you get used to it. Two years ago I broke my toe that way, and when you break a toe there isn't a thing you can do. So I just cut a hole in the shoe and taped it on like a football player. I was playing two days later.

Shin burgers are what we call the bruises you get from fouling balls off your legs. The black-and-blue mark lets people know you've been playing hard. Sometimes when you get hit in a meaty area you can see the stitch pattern of the ball on your skin, but if you can read the letters, there's something wrong. Because the letters on a ball aren't raised letters. But there have been times when people

have been hit so hard you can see the imprint of a letter. On one side of a National League ball is printed, "RO-A." Sometimes you can catch part of the "R." Not on a black guy though. You can see the seams on a black guy. But on a white guy if the ball catches him just right, you might see the letters.

One of our pitchers got a line drive back up the middle that bounced off his calf, and you could see the seams where it hit him. Then it turned black and blue, then purple. If it had been me, I'd have a little bruise where the ball hit me. But on this pitcher you could see where the blood sort of drained all the way down his whole leg. I said to him, "Man, you white guys bruise easy! Damn, Paul, I mean your whole leg is bruised up." So we have a lot of fun with it, but we all know it hurts. Nobody likes to get hit.

There are some guys in this league who will throw at heads. I just can't see that. Getting plunked in the hip or shoulder is part of the game. But there are a couple headhunters left in our game, and to me that's not right.

TONY GWYNN SCORES STANDING UP.

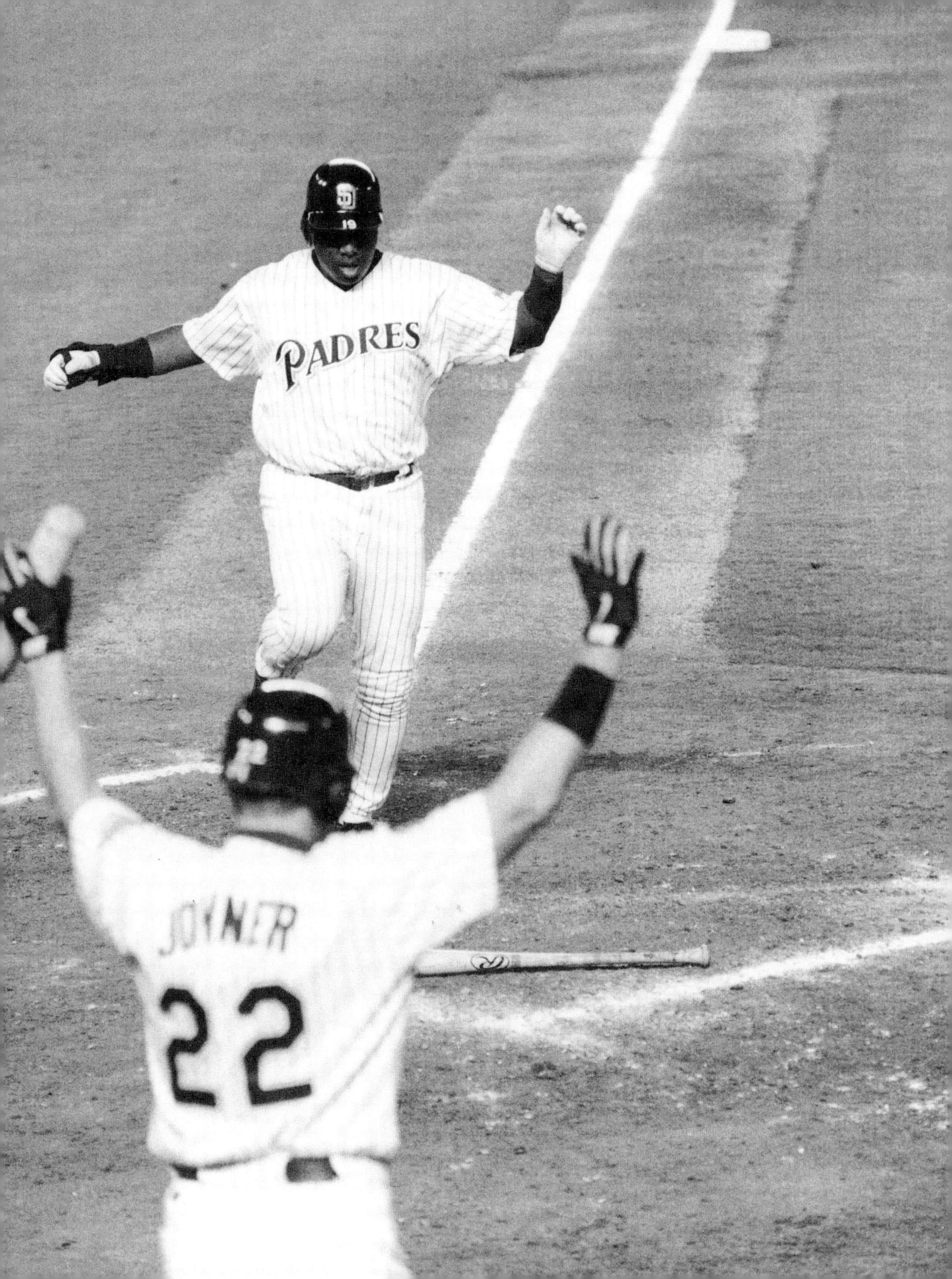
PADRES
JOYNER
22

LEARNING

THE BEST ARTISTS *never stop learning and growing. Tony Gwynn is testament to that. He not only works at his own art, hitting, but his baseball interests are comprehensive. He preaches the need to know yourself, and he advances his own quest every day. He knew when he got drafted into the majors*

that his fielding and base running were below par. So he studied, asked questions, observed, practiced. The result: five Gold Gloves, and more than 25 stolen bases over 5 seasons. Not bad for a guy who has described himself as "Old Blub."

As Gwynn has aged, he's made adjustments in conditioning, worked harder, and played smarter in order to be productive. And, together with Alicia, Tony is beginning to focus on off-the-field business.

KEN GRIFFEY, JR. "NOTE THE PLANTED FRONT FOOT AND THE STIFF FRONT LEG. THE RESULT: GREAT BALANCE. JUNIOR'S ONE OF THE BEST THERE IS."

Alicia's company, Gwynnsport, is making hay with Gwynn memorabilia and collectibles. The company's latest project is marketing Tony Gwynn bats, numbered from 1 to 372 (his 1997 National League Batting Championship average) that will sell for $450 each. And there are other deals on the table.

"I've got to hobnob," Tony said recently, with a smile. "Go see the employees of the companies I'm working for, shake their hands. I don't really like it all that much, but with the new ballpark issue coming up, I've got to get better at it. I can't just keep talking about baseball all the time. I've got to know what the heck's going on."

BARRY BONDS IN MID-SWING. AGAIN, NOTE THE STIFF FRONT LEG, BONDS' TOTAL CONTROL OF THE SITUATION.

Gwynn's list of company affiliations is already substantial: Franklin (sporting goods), Nike (shoes and clothing), Louisville Slugger (bats), Rawlings (gloves), and Oakley (sunglasses). Recently he *added Qualcomm, the San Diego telephone manufacturer, the company that bought the right to put its name on the Padres' home stadium in 1997.*

"Qualcomm is going to need some of my time during the season," Tony says with just a touch of apprehension. "I never would have done that in the past.

My season time was always sacred. But I feel I can do it now." Starting in November 1998, he'll be making commercials for Qualcomm. He was in the Qualcomm box during Super Bowl XXXII, meeting and greeting company guests.

The ballpark issue Gwynn refers to is the Padres' effort to build a new stadium in San Diego proper (the original Pacific

field," he protests, but he knows better. Tony Gwynn has always known what was going on

When I was in Walla Walla, Bobby Tolan told me the best thing to do was keep my mouth shut and my ears and eyes open. That's what I've always done. I realized early there is always going to be somebody on my team with more experi-

LEFT TO RIGHT: JEFF BAGWELL, MATTY ALOU, KENNY LOFTON.

Coast League Padres park, Lane Field, was on Harbor Drive in downtown San Diego). Gwynn fears he could become a pawn in the political game a voter referendum will stir up. "I just play right

ence than me, so why not pick their brain? If they're offering, why not listen?

I'm always observing other hitters, trying to find out how they do what they do. As a kid I followed Rod Carew, George Brett, Tony Oliva, Pete Rose, Matty Alou. They were my favorites. I liked the home-run guys, Brett and Oliva, but mostly I liked the guys who hit for average. When I was in Little League, I'd get the paper every day and look at the top ten. Those were the guys I related to and wanted to be like. I loved Willie Mays, Hank Aaron, and Harmon Killebrew, but I felt more on the same page with Rose and Carew.

The best thing about Interleague play in 1997 [for the first time, teams from the National and American Leagues played a schedule of games during the regular season] was that it gave me a chance to have a close look at a lot of good hitters I see only on television or maybe during spring training. Guys like Edgar Martinez, Mark McGwire, Ken Griffey, Jr., Garrett Anderson, and Jim Edmonds. That was great for me. I learned a lot that year. And I'm

ABOVE: **FRANK THOMAS. "NOTE HOW HIS FRONT FOOT IS OPENED UP."** RIGHT: **SAMMY SOSA. "HIS FRONT FOOT IS OPEN, TOO."** OPPOSITE: **GEORGE BRETT. "ALL THAT WEIGHT ON THE BACK FOOT. BUT HE MADE IT WORK. HE DID IT ALL: HIT FOR AVERAGE, HIT WITH POWER, STOLE BASES, AND WASN'T A BAD THIRD BASEMAN."**

sure they learned from watching me.

Having a chance to see Mark McGwire hit was instructive, because when you see him on television, you see a guy who is 6'6", 250 pounds, with a ton of power. But the thing I learned about McGwire is that he's a contact hitter! He's not looking to go up there and juice the ball every

time, pull it out of the park. He turns his legs in until he's almost pigeon-toed, which helps him keep his balance and his weight back. He doesn't really try to muscle the ball. He hits it out because when he connects with a good swing he's got all that power. But he's basically a contact hitter, and you would only know that from watching him close up.

One of the best exhibitions of hitting I saw during the 1997 season was from Ken Griffey, Jr. For our first Interleague game in Seattle, we went to the Kingdome. It was my first time playing there, so I got to the park early just to have a look around. Griffey was on the field at 2:30 P.M., five hours before game time, taking extra hits. He wasn't trying to launch every pitch into the right field stands. In fact he was working on hitting every ball to the left side of second base.

His first time up that night, Griffey got hold of a fastball out over the plate: Pow, it was gone, left center. Because I had watched him practice, I wasn't surprised.

OPPOSITE: **EDGAR MARTINEZ.** "HE'S GOT THE BAT WRAPPED AROUND HIS HEAD, BUT HE GETS IT TO THE HITTING POSITION." RIGHT: **GARRETT ANDERSON** (TOP) AND **JIM EDMONDS.**

ABOVE: **BARRY BONDS MAKING SOMETHING HAPPEN WITH WHAT HE'S BEEN GIVEN.**
OPPOSITE: **MIKE PIAZZA GETS ALL OF ONE.**

Next time up, fastball in—gone, right center. Third time up there's a runner on first, two outs. You know we weren't playing shallow to cut off the run, not with Griffey up. In fact, we backed up. Pow—double in the gap, left center, he knocks in the run. So he's three for three: homer to right center, homer to left center, and a double to left center.

His next at-bat he waited on a pitch, and hit a double down the left-field line. Three of his four hits were to left because that's what he intended to do, that's what he practiced.

Edgar Martinez is the same kind of hitter as McGwire and Griffey. He's a student of the art, willing to take what he is given and make something of it. Every now and then he'll get a ball in the zone and do damage. Make a mistake with Martinez and he'll hit it out. The best hitters always make a pitcher pay for a mistake. Martinez, Griffey, McGwire, Bonds—they'll bust you if you make a mistake. They're complete hitters.

The Angels' Garrett Anderson is

smooth. He's not a big home-run hitter, but he's got a chance to be in that category. He's got a fluid swing with lots of pop. Pitchers have to be careful with him. He's just learning how good he can be. In 1997, he was off and on. He's got to fine tune, learn to be consistent.

Jim Edmonds is like Anderson only with more pop. He's a freer swinger with more power and hits a lot of home runs to the opposite field. Make a mistake out over the plate with Edmonds and he'll bust you. But he won't make something out of what you give him all the time. He's too eager to hit the ball out. He needs more patience.

Observing is good, but talking with other players is the best. I'm a talkative type, so when I get on first I usually start a conversation with the first baseman. I talk with catchers and umpires too, although sometimes I feel uncomfortable about it because the anti-fraternization rule is in effect. From 15 minutes before the game begins until it ends you're not supposed to fraternize with the opposition. But guys want to pick your brain, I want to pick their brain, so you do what you have to do.

And you don't get to see the other players that often, outside of a game situation. When a guy is hitting well, I want to ask him how he feels, how he did this or that. So if I get a base hit, the first baseman comes over to hold me on, and I just start talking with him.

It was difficult when I was younger. Some of the older guys didn't want to talk to me or help me out because they thought I was after their jobs. But among the established players there is no hesitancy. It's a fair exchange.

One of the best conversations I had in 1997 was at the All-Star game. Kenny Lofton, Moises Alou, and Barry Larkin were sitting at a table in the clubhouse talking about hitting. I came in from the field and they called me over and asked me a question about hitting the ball the other way. Before long there were 12 guys standing around the table talking about hitting. The pitchers were throwing in their two cents—Darryl Kile, Curt Schilling, Kevin Brown.

I remember I said that experience is the thing. Experience helps you become a

WALLY JOYNER IN THE MOMENT BETWEEN CONTACT AND SPRINTING OUT OF THE BOX. GOOD CONCENTRATION, GOOD BALANCE.

better hitter at this level because we face the same guys so many times. It works both ways. Pitchers face hitters, hitters face pitchers. Pitchers have ideas about how they're going to attack hitters and vice versa. Every now and then you run into that one guy—and I was looking at Kevin Brown—whose stuff is electric. He's got the power sinker, he's got the power slider, his ball runs, and you can't go up there looking for something particular off a guy like that. You've got to react to what you see. You won't be successful waiting for him to hang a slider, because if he's throwing a power sinker for a strike, you won't hit it.

By the time we finished, there were a bunch of pitchers—Neagle, Maddox, Pedro Martinez—and a few other hitters. Frank Robinson was there, too. This is a situation where you can learn a lot about hitting simply by sitting around and talking to your peers.

There were also a couple of guys there who were on the All-Star team for the first time. They weren't saying anything, but they were sure enough taking it all in.

MARK McGWIRE, CONTACT HITTER WITH POWER.

And that's what it's all about. When I go around the league, other hitters who want me to sign a ball or a bat sometimes send the ballboy over with it. When that happens I send the ballboy right back with a message: if he wants a ball, tell him to come and ask me. Tell him to come over and have a conversation. First of all, both of us might learn something, and he'll remember it a lot more if I sign it and hand it to him. I guess I embarrass a lot of people by doing that.

We went to Anaheim for our first Interleague game, and sure enough, Garrett Anderson and Jimmy Edmonds sent the ballboy over to see me. And I told the ballboy, hey man, those guys see me out there taking batting practice, and I'm out there watching them taking batting practice. Just tell them to come over and ask for it. And so after batting practice they wandered over, "Hey, Mr. Gwynn, I appreciate you signing the ball for me." The next thing you know we're talking about hitting. If they ask me, I tell them what I think. But I'm not heavy, I don't try to tell them how to do their jobs. I just throw stuff out and move on.

It's great to make the All-Star team, but the best part about it isn't the game itself, it's the opportunity to talk about baseball with the top players. I've been to 13 All-Star games, and I remember 11 of them for the conversations I had. In 1986 I went to the All-Star game in Oakland and I didn't start. I pinch-hit in the second inning and I was done.

But that All-Star game sticks out in my mind because I had a great time just sitting on the bench talking with Dave Parker and Tim Raines about hitting. Dave Parker is one of the funniest human beings I've ever known. And Rock Raines is the same way.

It sucked as far as what I contributed to the All-Star game, because I grounded out on two pitches against Bret Saberhagen. But sitting on the bench made it all worthwhile. The game went 14 innings until Tim Raines got the base hit that won it for the National League.

I was a young guy when I played my first All-Star game in 1984, and I was scared to death. Dale Murphy started in center, Mike Schmidt started at third, Steve Garvey was at first. With Mike Schmidt, ego never got in the way. If you had a question, he would give you the best answer he could.

Another guy like that was Ozzie Smith.

I played with Ozzie in I don't know how many All-Star games, and my locker was always next to his—probably because we were the oldest guys on the National League side. We would just sit there for hours yakking about baseball. We talked about hits, we talked about stealing bases. I know nothing about playing the infield, but when Ozzie was talking with Barry Larkin about playing shortstop, exchanging little tricks of the trade, I'd sit there and soak it all up. Even though it didn't apply to me, I was still taking it in.

I think that one of my jobs as an experienced All-Star player is to make the younger guys realize how important that event is. Some players treat the All-Star game like it's a vacation; I go to the All-Star game to try to help my side win. I also try to make the younger players feel at ease, because suddenly they're alongside players they've watched as kids. A lot of times they feel uncomfortable. I remember how uncomfortable I felt when I made it the first time.

OPENING CEREMONIES OF THE ALL-STAR GAME IN SAN FRANCISCO IN 1984, GWYNN'S FIRST. "I WAS SCARED TO DEATH THAT DAY, BUT I GOT A HIT AND STOLE A BASE."

GOING BAD

EVERYBODY HAS GOOD *days and bad days. It's when the bad days stack up back-to-back that anxiety sets in. It can escalate to panic, followed by depression. When it comes to hitting a baseball, this situation is called a "slump." It is so integral to a baseball player's experience that in defining the word, Webster's Tenth Edition New Collegiate Dictionary quotes Ted Williams: "One spring I was in a batting slump."*

The major characteristic of a slump is the gut-wrenching feeling that it could be permanent. It's as perplexing as it is maddening. How can an ability that has brought one a certain amount of success simply disappear in the night without a trace? Like car keys that are missing from all the usual places when you're packed and ready to leave for the airport, a slump refuses to respond to tried and true techniques. At the plate you can feel as balanced as the Parthenon; concentrate with the focus of Mt. Palomar Observatory's telescope on the pitcher's release point; land softly as a butterfly on the ball of the front foot; get your hands to the picture-perfect hitting position; bring the knob of the bat oh-so-smartly to the ball; and end up with a follow-through that would put a computer model to shame—and you still can't connect properly with the ball. A slump is enough to drive the most rational hitter beyond distraction. Gwynn knows. He's suffered his share of slumps.

A batting slump starts with the physical side, but as it progresses, it quickly becomes a mental problem—and it gets worse if you start thinking too much.

That's why you hear a lot of hitters say that when they go to the plate they don't want to think, they want to react. When you start thinking, you usually start guessing. And if you're guessing, and you're wrong, you're making a lot of outs. And even if you're guessing right, you're going to make outs. It gets back to knowing yourself. You have to know what you do, and why you do it.

You enter a slump because even though you might know what you're doing wrong, you just can't seem to correct it. You can't find the one thing that's going to allow you to get back into a hitting groove. What I do in that situation is backtrack, go back to the basics. First and foremost is the video. I put all my hits on one tape. When I'm going good I don't look at that tape too much. When I'm going bad I look at it a lot. I check the mechanics of my swing from a couple of weeks before I started going bad to where I am at the moment. And it's funny, there are times when I'm getting hits regularly despite not swinging the bat very well. Because of all the years I've worked at this game and because I know myself so well, I can get away with making mistakes. But I won't be happy about it.

When I hit a slump it's usually a problem with my balance. I get my weight on the front foot and play pepper with the second baseman. I had a streak in 1997 when I grounded out 12 straight times to the second baseman. Because when you land hard on the front foot, your weight shifts before you swing the bat. The weight pulls your bat around too soon and you hit the ball out in front. Result: grounder to second.

So I get out the batting tee and whiffle ball. I work at this until the knuckle balls are coming off the tee one after another. But sometimes what it takes is one at-bat doing it right to get you back in the direction you want to go. Sometimes it's just the way you take a pitch. Sometimes it's a casual remark somebody makes that triggers a solution. It can be an out as well as a hit, if you suddenly get the feel of the bat back.

A slump can bring up all the other stuff in life that's ever bothered you. There were times in my first half-dozen seasons when I'd hole myself up in my

"IN THE ON-DECK CIRCLE DURING A SLUMP, IT FEELS LIKE YOU'RE ABOUT TO BE FED TO THE LIONS."

DURING A SLUMP, GWYNN LIKES TO STUDY HIS "GREATEST HITS" VIDEOTAPES TO SEE WHAT HE WAS DOING RIGHT.

room and wouldn't talk to anybody. It's painful to recall those slumps. I was so bad that my kids would slide off to bed before I got home. It's because I took the game so seriously. When I failed, I brought the game home, and that was a mistake.

Mentally, the challenge of a slump is to find a way not to be frustrated, and to figure a way out of it. It helps if you have

gone through a slump and come out of it. Then you know that no matter how badly you're doing, it will pass.

My breakthrough about slumps came in the 1988 season. I started out terrible. A week before the All-Star break I was hitting .233. I was desperate to fix it. Finally I just admitted to myself, and I told Alicia, "I suck. I just suck right now. I don't have to sit here and try to explain why I suck. I just know I suck." I came to terms with it and decided I had to gradually work my way out of it.

I came home the next night after going

0 for 4 again, and I just let go of all the tension and pressure of not getting hits. The next night, I went 2 for 3, but they were ugly hits.

Bob Walker was pitching for the Pirates. He had me one and two. He threw me a fastball tailing away and I lined it between short and third for a base hit. It was the first time in about two months that I had done that. And that was the hit that got me on track. I went home that night and told Alicia that I thought I'd found something. Although I was hitting .233 at the time, I hit .360 in the second half of the season and won the batting title. I had a great come-from-behind second half. I shouldn't have won that title, but I did, because I stopped being my worst enemy.

I learned a valuable lesson that year: There are times during the course of a season where you just have to admit that you suck. The public admission is what takes all the pressure off. Everybody knows you suck now, and you can be free to start all over again and try to do things right.

I'm not sure you can teach this to a younger player. I think you have to have some experience before you can really understand what I'm talking about. You have to endure some slumps and battle your way out of them. Because at the minor league level a guy's slump isn't that prominent. It might be in the local paper, but it's not national news. When I go 4 for 40, I'm on that "Who's Not" list on ESPN's Who's Hot and Who's Not.

STRIKE THREE

Frequent strike-outs go with slumps. I hate to strike out more than anything, especially when there's some young guy on the hill who gets all cranked because he struck out Tony Gwynn.

Striking out once in a while is tolerable because it's unavoidable. Once in a game is bad enough, but twice is tough. I once struck out three times in one night, when Bob Welch of the Dodgers was pitching. It was headline news. I got mad about it. They don't do that with anybody else. But it's a hole I dug for myself; if you usually don't strike out a lot and you strike out a couple of times in a game, it's big news.

Even if I'm not in a slump, there's still the day-to-day frustration you have to deal with. Striking out swinging is what I hate the most. Most guys feel the dumbest when they get called out with the bat on their shoulder. I hate swinging and

VIDEO

The Padres were the last team in major league baseball to have a video room. Before the new owners took over in 1990, we had a regular VCR, and the tapes were bad. It wasn't good enough for us to do what we had to do. So I said, "Forget it, I'll buy a video setup." It cost me eighty-five grand. We're plugged into the video feeds from the game cameras.

It's set up in the clubhouse. Now there are so many guys using it you have to make an appointment to get in there to look at stuff. Because I bought it, I make the rules. The other guys can look all they want, but if I have to look at something, well, that's the way it goes.

It's a good system. I can lead off an inning, make an out, come inside, and look at that at-bat before I go out and play defense, which I do a lot. Our video guy, Mike Halder, has been on the job since we got the equipment. He remarked recently that I don't come up to look at the hits anymore. He said I just looked at the outs. He was right. If I get a hit I figure I must have done something right. So I can wait until I get home to see that. But if I make an out, I want to see what I did wrong.

During the season, I look at the video every day. I have an at-bat tape that includes every pitch of every at-bat. That shows me what the pitcher tried to do, and how I responded. Then I have a hit tape that strings the hits together. Either Mike or I put these together. Before we got the video equipment I'd set up my little video machine, tape the ballgame, and then take my at-bats off that game tape and put it on my hit tape, if I got any hits. I've been doing that since 1983.

I take two little portable machines with me on the road. As soon as I get to the hotel, the first thing I do is watch the tapes. The "oh-for" nights are still hard to look at. I hate looking at outs. I don't mind looking at outs if I'm doing things right, but if not it's ugly. Guess you have to take the good with the bad.

missing because I feel so awkward, like I've really made an ass of myself. Striking out swinging means I've been fooled, and I feel like a goat going back to the dugout, especially at Dodger Stadium where it's a long walk and the fans have plenty of time to rag you.

On those days, when I get in my car to drive home, I open all the windows and the sunroof, and I yell at the top of my lungs, "Aiiiiiiiiii Suuuuuuuuuuuk!" Then I close the windows, turn up the music, and I'm fine.

Merv Rettenmund, our hitting coach, has a good theory about sucking. He says, maybe you're not sucking; maybe you're just going real good. The young guys ask him what he means. He says, maybe you're not sucking right now. Maybe you're going great and it's gonna get worse. They look at him cross-eyed. He tells them, hey, it can get a lot worse.

I remember one time—the year I should have won the batting title when I hurt my knee—the doctors gave me a cortisone

GWYNN RESTS IN THE DUGOUT DURING EARLY BATTING PRACTICE, FOUR HOURS BEFORE A GAME.

shot and I had to take three days off. When I came back my knee felt great. That had been my problem hitting. I couldn't push off my back leg because of knee pain.

I was taking extra hitting one day and I told Merv, "You know what? I've found it." And he said, "You've found it? Man oh man, T's found it. Hey, hey." Greg Riddoch, the manager that year, took up the cry. He said, "Hey, Tony's found it. Keep that in mind today when the game starts."

When the game started I was doing the same thing as before. I was drifting forward like I'd been doing. I made an out, came back to the bench and Merv looked at me and said, "Yeah, T, you found it all right." And he still rags me today about how I found it. I'll never say that again.

GWYNN GOING TO WORK IN THE TUNNEL THAT LEADS TO THE HOME TEAM DUGOUT AT QUALCOMM STADIUM, OR "THE Q."

OLD SCHOOL

ECAUSE FREE AGENCY *has bred so much team-hopping, one forgets how baseball teams and their name players used to be synonymous with the cities that supported them. Remember the Pittsburgh Pirates, 1979? "We Are Family," by Sister Sledge, was the stirring song of that great Pirates*

season. Willie "Pops" Stargell and Dave Parker were *the Pittsburgh Pirates.*

Beyond that, Richie Ashburn, Mike Schmidt, and Steve Carlton were the Philadelphia Phillies; Pete Rose, Johnny Bench, and Joe Morgan were the Cincinnati Reds; Duke Snyder, Don Drysdale, and Sandy Koufax were the Los Angeles Dodgers; Jim Palmer, Brooks Robinson, and Cal Ripkin were the Baltimore Orioles; and Whitey Ford, Roger Maris, and Mickey Mantle (to mention three) were the New York Yankees. One can only imagine the outcry if any of those teams even considered trading one of those players.

Today, no team or city loyalty can pre-

vent most players from chasing the big money around the league. Baseball families are kaput. Each season brings on a new set of faces. If you're not a regular at the local ballpark, you might glance at the starting lineup and think you've wandered into the All-Star game. The guy you loved to hate last year is now playing for your team.

That's why players like Tony Gwynn are so unique, and such valuable commodities. At a time when fan confusion is at an all-time high, Gwynn (16 seasons with the Padres) and his East Coast confederate, Cal Ripken (17 seasons with the Orioles), swim happily against the

tide, providing continuity and stability. They also continue to play good, competitive baseball.

Both Gwynn and Ripken long ago got the keys to their cities, and both have used them well. Getting Tony Gwynn to talk about his civic contributions is like pulling teeth, and that's part of the attraction. His considerable charity work is done without fanfare. He feels it's just part of being a responsible citizen.

Padres President and CEO, Larry Lucchino, says Gwynn isn't "from" San Diego, he is "of" San Diego. "The value of his loyalty and identity is incalculable," Lucchino says. "We all need heroes, and San Diego has a hero in Tony Gwynn. He's repaid the city for its adulation with his commitment, and everyone knows it. Gwynn is a throwback to the way things used to be, when players were an essential part of a city's fabric."

San Diego is Gwynn's home for the duration. The Padres, for better or for worse, are his extended family. He wouldn't have it any other way.

A lot of people think I'm crazy to stay in San Diego with the Padres. My dad

MR. AND MRS. TONY GWYNN.

was one of them. I argued with him about that two days before he died. He wanted me to pack my bags and get the hell out of San Diego. I told him I'm happy, I like it here. I said that things will turn around soon for the team. But we had just traded McGriff and Sheffield, and he was angry. He thought I should leave because the Padres weren't trying to win. I had to agree with him about that, but I just told him that I'm happy in San Diego.

You go to work, and when work's over you get in your car and drive home. If you're happy, if you like your situation, that means a lot. It means a little bit more than just being able to collect a paycheck on the first of every month. And even though I wasn't in the optimum financial position, I knew I'd continue to be happy here. That's why I'm still here.

It also means something to be able to play your whole career for one team. I really wanted to do that, right from the beginning. I'm an old-fashioned guy. They call it "old school" now. I really wanted to play all my career with the Padres. The guy who's leading the way in that category is Baltimore's Cal Ripken. He's got the longest tenure on one team. But I'm right behind him.

Team-jumping is about ego as much as money. You want to be the highest-paid guy in baseball, or you at least want to rank in the top 10. Early in my career that was important to me. I felt that I was worthy of being in the top 20, maybe even the top 10. Now here I am, 37 years old, I've just won my eighth batting title, and I doubt if I'm in the top 50. Does that bother me? Not at all, because I'm happy. I have enough, on the one hand. On the other hand, I'm greedy like anybody else. I'd like more. But the Padres offered me enough to stay and I took it.

I have three years left on my contract extension. I'll be 40 when I retire. And there are a few things I care about other than money. Getting my 3,000th hit is important to me. This contract gives me that opportunity. And I don't have to worry about being traded or being drafted in the expansion draft because I'm a ten-and-five guy; ten years in the big leagues and at least five years on the same club, so I have veto power. The Padres can't trade me. I can't be drafted. I've earned the right to stay here. But I don't want to stay somewhere I'm not wanted.

Right now the Padres want me. But it's a constant challenge. It's a motivational thing. This is where I want to be, but at the same time I want them to want me here because I do my job. That's what keeps me working hard to be productive. I don't want to be put in a position where they might want me to retire, or agree to a trade. I want to go out on my own terms. Not a lot of guys get to play with teams long enough to do that. But that's one of the luxuries I've worked toward. If I just want to shut it down in the middle of the season, I could do that. Because I've earned the right. But that's not my way. If I go to spring training and I suck and don't improve, then I'll pack it in.

My attitude about staying in San Diego doesn't exactly make me the darling of the Major League Players Association. The animosity between us started early in my career. I signed a six-year deal at the end of the 1984 season for $4.6 million. The Association was highly upset because they felt I was underpaid. One night the pastor of Alicia's church and her husband were in our house, and I was on the telephone arguing with Gene Orza from the Association. I said, "Gene, how can you sit at a desk in New York and tell me what I should sign for?" He said, "Well, I've got over 700 players that I

THE GREATER GWYNN FAMILY AT HOME (LEFT TO RIGHT): DAUGHTER ANISHA, 12; NIECE TYNISE CURETON, 17; TONY; ALICIA; SON ANTHONY, 15; AND NEPHEW CHASANT BYRD, 15.

have to look out for." I said, "Fine, look out for them. I'm looking out for Tony Gwynn and his family." And he just started cursing at me because I signed. I said, "Get the hell out of my business."

I don't talk to him any more. Players call the Association to get information on who's making what. I can't be bothered. I don't compare myself with other players, but in 1984 the Association was comparing me to Steve Sax, Tim Raines, Brett Butler, Willie McGee, and others. They all were making more money than me. But I

was a security guy. If the Padres offered me something with some security where I could buy my family a house, I was going to take it. So when they offered that contract, I jumped on it. Orza and I went 'round and 'round on the phone. He cussed me out. I cussed him out. I said,

"Gene, you can sit up there and cuss all you want to. The bottom line is I signed." He said, "No, the bottom line is we haven't approved it." I said, "Well, what? You aren't going to approve it?"

The Association has to approve player contracts, so does the League. Today they don't put the heat on the player, they put the heat on the agent. They can't control the player, but they can control the agent. In Major League baseball the agents have to be certified by the Association. If it doesn't like the way an agent is doing business, it can pull his certification. As a result, most agents end up giving in and try to get their players to do what the Association wants.

If that's how they want to operate, fine. But my agent knows how I operate. We don't even deal with the Association. They know I could have been a free agent at the end of 1997 and gone out in the open market and commanded some heavy money, but I know the Padres couldn't afford to match it.

Barry Bonds was getting an extension in San Francisco, Gary Sheffield was about to sign with the Marlins, Sammy Sosa would be signing with the Cubs. And their prices were high. If those guys are worth ten million a year, I could have gotten six or seven. Ripken had signed an extension for $6.3 a year, and when I signed my extension I told the Padres that I would never get to the point where I would become a free agent and actually test the market to see what I'm worth. But Ripken's extension is worth $18 million for three years. That's what I figured I'd be looking at on the market. But the Padres couldn't afford to pay me Ripken dollars. So I said, I'm trying to be fair. I'm giving you guys an opportunity to lock me up. I know how important I am to the community of San Diego. I just threw it out there. I said, look, you guys are never going to get a new ballpark without me. I know that, you know that. Ripken has signed a three-year extension and we both know what he's making. I deserve a raise. I'm making $4 million right now. I deserve a raise. I'm not saying how much. I'm just telling you I deserve a raise.

Going into the negotiation I had told my agent if they offered me the same thing that I'm making I'd take it. We went in, and we didn't get anywhere. We talked for about four or five days. Finally, I said, give me a raise and I'll sign and I'll stay. Very simple. The next day we got it done. I got a nice $300,000 raise from what I was making, which was $300,000 more than I really wanted. Yet I'm the fool. I'm crazy for signing a three-year extension worth $12.9 million. Because Sheffield and Sosa are getting so much more.

Those guys are certainly happy with the money they have. Whether or not they're happy in the situations they're in, I can't tell you. I do know that it would make no sense for me to go to New York or anywhere else for a couple million dollars more a year when all of my ties are in San Diego. I've gladly taken less money to be where I'm happy.

The Gwynn's invited me over to watch game three of the 1997 World Series. It was being played in Cleveland in bitter cold and occasional blizzard conditions. Tony wasn't back from having an MRI on his knees. He feared that surgery—his fourth procedure in 16 seasons—was going to be necessary. The large, Spanish-style house was bustling with the Gwynn's two children and a live-in niece and nephew who range in age from 12 to 16, half a dozen assorted friends and relatives, and a seamstress who had come by to do some fittings. Alicia made introductions, then pointed me toward the big television in the living room.

Tony came charging in halfway through the second inning with good news: only one knee needed surgery. He'd been wondering if he'd have to have both knees done, and he was obviously relieved. "No sweat. Arthroscopic procedure, in and out in one day, begin easy workouts in two weeks."

Alicia served some chicken she'd whipped up in her gourmet kitchen. We took our plates into the living room and settled down to watch the game. Tony got rolling like the comprehensive analyst he

is. He's part historian, part color commentator. His memory is amazing, and he's accurate right down to the spelling of Hideo Nomo's first name. He misses nothing, even with the television cameras providing his only vantage points.

Pitching is always tougher in the Series. The hitters are better, and there's more concentration. You see fewer balls thrown over the middle of the plate during the Series.

The cold hurts batters on the outside and inside pitches. Hitting the ball on the handle or the end of the bat smarts. After fouling one off the end of the bat it takes an inning-and-a-half to get the feeling back in your hands.

Bobby Bonilla is in tough shape. His hamstring is really sore. Look at the shoes. Patent leather. I was the first to have those. I had a pair made for me because they're a lot lighter.

"Bip" Roberts. They're saying that was a childhood nickname. No way. You

GWYNN'S PATENT LEATHERS. "IT TOOK ME UNTIL 1997 TO GET STYLISH SHOES. THEY'RE ALSO LIGHTER AND MORE COMFORTABLE. I HAD THEM PUT '5.5 HOLE' ON THE TONGUE TO REMIND ME HOW I MAKE MY LIVING."

FANS

The job of the opposition's fans is to distract you, take your mind off the game. So they rag you to death. They call you every name in the book. It doesn't get racial very often. It's just the fans' way of trying to get you off your game.

Chicago, Wrigley Field, is pretty bad. But I still get respect there. A few years ago, I went five-for-five in a game there. They gave me a standing ovation when I ran off the field. It was pretty awesome. For most of the other games, though, they were on my case.

In general, the San Diego fans have been really good to me because I think they respect what I do, respect the way I go about my business, respect the fact I've been loyal to the Padres. But if you start not doing your job, they're going to be on your case.

West Coast fans are more laid back, not as boisterous, not as nasty. The further east you go, the worse it gets. St. Louis has got the arch, they call it the Gateway, and that's right. It's the gateway to the more knowledgeable fan. In St. Louis they know what's going on.

The fans are not only more knowledgeable, but they're louder the further east you go. On the West Coast, baseball games are more like a happening. If the team you're playing is playing well, the fans come out because the ball park is a happening place to be. They don't necessarily get into the strategy of the game.

In the East, they know. You go into New York, Pittsburgh, or Philadelphia, they know how the game is supposed to be played. They second-guess the manager, they're letting you know how they feel about everything that happens. Basically the fans have been great to me. They rag me but at least they still respect what I do.

Then there's Canada. You have to experience the Canadian baseball fans to believe them, I think. You're out there playing, and maybe their team has a great rally going, and the place is silent. They don't go after foul balls like American fans. If you catch it, you catch it. If you don't, that's okay. Not that

they're not knowledgeable, because I think they are. But really what's on their minds is hockey. They go to the baseball game today because there's no hockey game until tomorrow. They truly love hockey.

know how he got that? Because every spring training he would get hurt. One day a teammate says, that guy was born in pain. Born - in - pain. B - i - p. It stuck.

Behind us, a display of trophies takes up an entire wall. Uniform shirts, autographed balls, Gold Gloves, Silver Slugger awards for being best at your position, and the collection of full-size sterling silver bats, trophies for winning the National League batting championship. Seven of them. The eighth won't arrive until the beginning of the next season. The bats are in varying stages of tarnish, which is Gwynn's preference.

After five innings, Cleveland jumped to a five-run lead. Tony led the way to his "closet," a sizable room off the master bedroom he calls his dungeon. Surrounded by racks of warm-up suits and sneakers, we pulled up chairs in front of two small television monitors and looked at one of Tony's "hit" videos. He has at-bat tapes that chronicle every pitch of every at-bat. From those, he copies the outs onto one tape, the hits onto another. He

says he likes watching the hit tape because it shows him doing things right. He says the hit tapes are the best medicine for a slump. As hit after hit flew by, Gwynn narrated.

Inside ball, double to right. Look outside, react inside, that's how it works.

Here's one of me hitting down on a high pitch. It's hard to do, but you can't swing up on a high ball. You'll never catch up with it.

A home run off Nomo. I know if the fork ball isn't working, look for the heater inside. I managed to turn on it. Home run.

Here's Candiotti. Knuckle baller. All the rules are off. Just try to hit the thing. Forget about the front foot down softly, forget about everything. Good luck to the batter *and* the catcher.

Oh yeah, inside the park home run, *and* a grand slam. I've got two inside the park homers lifetime. And people say I can't run (he laughs). Gee, there are a lot of home runs on this tape. I want you to know I just grabbed this tape at random (more laughter).

Here's a really high pitch, up around the shoulders, but see how I still manage to hit down on it. I look at that and wonder how I do it. It comes naturally, *and* I work at it.

Florida had gotten two runs in the sixth inning, cutting Cleveland's lead to 7-5. The phone rang. Tony picked it up and started talking about his upcoming knee surgery to a friend. Cleveland's first baseman, Jim Thome, lined a ball up the middle. Earlier, Gwynn had been talking about Thome, who had been struggling. Now he asked his caller to wait, put his hand over the phone and said, "You see that? His foot landed, his hands were there, his balance was good. All he had left to do was swing the bat."

Gwynn went back to his call, then said goodbye and hung up.

Thome was overdue, I believe in that. But you still have to do it right. Hitting is about getting in a balanced position every time.

Gwynn paused. Took a pull on his soda.

You know, there's nothing better than the sound of a bat on a ball.

GWYNN POSES WITH PRIDE AT THE BALLFIELD NAMED AFTER HIM AT SAN DIEGO STATE, HIS ALMA MATER. TONY GWYNN FIELD WAS COMPLETED IN 1997.

PHOTO CREDITS